THEOSOMNIA

of related interest

Interreligious Dialogue and the Partition of India
Hindus and Muslims in Dialogue about Violence and Forced Migration
Mario I. Aguilar
ISBN 978 1 78592 312 8
eISBN 978 1 78450 625 4
Studies in Religion and Theology

Exploring Moral Injury in Sacred Texts
Edited by Joseph McDonald
Foreword by Rita Nakashima Brock
ISBN 978 1 78592 756 0
eISBN 978 1 78450 591 2
Studies in Religion and Theology

God Beyond Words
Christian Theology and the Spiritual Experiences of
People with Profound Intellectual Disabilities
Jill Harshaw
ISBN 978 1 78592 044 8
eISBN 978 1 78450 302 4
Studies in Religion and Theology

Christian Ashrams, Hindu Caves and Sacred Rivers
Christian-Hindu Monastic Dialogue in India 1950–1993
Mario I. Aguilar
ISBN 978 1 78592 086 8
eISBN 978 1 78450 347 5
Studies in Religion and Theology

Performing Pastoral Care
Music as a Framework for Exploring Pastoral Care
Gregory Clifton-Smith
ISBN 978 1 78592 036 3
eISBN 978 1 78450 287 4
Studies in Religion and Theology

THEOSOMNIA
A Christian Theology of Sleep

Andrew Bishop

Jessica Kingsley *Publishers*
London and Philadelphia

First published in 2018
by Jessica Kingsley Publishers
73 Collier Street
London N1 9BE, UK
and
400 Market Street, Suite 400
Philadelphia, PA 19106, USA

www.jkp.com

Library of Congress Cataloging in Publication Data
Names: Bishop, Andrew (Canon), author.
Title: Theosomnia : explorations in theology and sleep / Andrew Bishop.
Description: Philadelphia : Jessica Kingsley Publishers, 2018.
Identifiers: LCCN 2017045819 | ISBN 9781785922183
Subjects: LCSH: Sleep--Religious aspects--Christianity.
Classification: LCC BT741.3 .B57 2018 | DDC 233--dc23 LC
record available at https://lccn.loc.gov/2017045819

British Library Cataloguing in Publication Data
A CIP catalogue record for this book is available from the British Library

ISBN 978 1 78592 218 3
eISBN 978 1 78450 495 3

Printed and bound in the United States

In thanksgiving for the life of
Geoffrey Douglas Rowell, Bishop (1943–2017),
who encouraged me in my writing and thinking and
who, sadly, never saw this work completed.

Almighty God and Father,
it is our certain faith that your Son,
who died on the cross, was raised from the dead,
the first-fruits of all who have fallen asleep.

Grant that through this mystery
your servant and bishop Geoffrey,
who has gone to his rest in Christ,
may share in the joy of his resurrection.

We ask this Christ our Lord.

Amen.

CONTENTS

ACKNOWLEDGEMENTS

My interest in theology and sleep was prompted by my chance attendance in May 2013 at an interdisciplinary roundtable event at the University of Surrey. As Anglican and Coordinating Chaplain at the University I enjoy hearing about academic endeavours along with the customary pastoral work of a chaplain. Subsequent conversations with academics at the University, amongst them Dr Rob Meadows and Professor Annette Steer, inspired me to think further on this subject. Dr Michael Greaney of Lancaster University encouraged me to write for the academic blog www.sleepcultures.com, and I have had stimulating email exchanges and conversations with Dr Garret Sullivan of Pennsylvania State University. I am indebted to them for their generosity towards me as an academic interloper.

It was my Extended Ministerial Development Leave (sabbatical) in 2015 from the University and Guildford Cathedral, where I am a Residentiary Canon, that gave me an opportunity to think further and write on the subject. Throughout this time colleagues at the University and Cathedral have been interested and encouraging. Canon Dr Julie Gittoes has been characteristically supportive and generous in conversation about the subject. It was Julie who originally put me in touch with Natalie Watson, at Jessica Kingsley Publishers, who then took the risk of commissioning this book and has been encouraging in her guidance and support. I am indebted to Katherine Dienes-Williams, Organist and Master of the Choristers at Guildford Cathedral, for introducing me to both Sir Thomas Browne's prayer, which I draw on heavily in this book, and the setting of it by Sir William Harris (1883–1973), which I first came across at Choral Evensong in the Cathedral. I have also had the opportunity afforded by invitations from parishes and other church networks around the Diocese of Guildford to lead study and quiet days that has set the academic dimension in this work to its proper service as far as a theologian should be concerned, which is the life of the Church.

My early reflections formed the basis of my leading the annual Westminster Abbey Day of Prayer on the subject in 2014. A particular honour was to be invited by Abbot Giles Hill, OSB, to lead the community retreat for the Abbey of Our Lady and St John, Alton, Hampshire, in September 2016. It is in that precious and holy place that I began writing this book in earnest. I am also deeply grateful to my brother-in-law, Professor Peter Hunt, for reading the final manuscript and making helpful comments that have improved the final product. It goes without saying that all shortcomings are very much my own. Finally my thanks are due, as ever, to my family. My wife, Alice, is a devotee of sleep. At a young age our children, Edmund, Charles, Hugh and Beatrice, all disrupted our sleep in varying degrees, but now as they get older themselves find that they sleep more than we do – one of the curious features of sleep at different ages and stages of life. I want to thank them from the bottom of my heart, especially when time that might have been spent with them has gone into this book. I hope they are proud of it and that you, the reader, enjoy it.

Andrew Bishop
The Falling Asleep of the Mother of God

Note on the text

Biblical quotations unless otherwise stated are from the *New Revised Standard Version (NRSV)*.

INTRODUCTION

The study of sleep has become a field of widespread interest. It engages many disciplines from neuroscience to sociology, and from philosophy to evolutionary biology. It features in the lifestyle sections of newspapers and websites often because of its connections with mental and physical wellbeing. Yet theology has, in the most part, remained silent on the subject despite many biblical references to sleep in both the Old and New Testaments.

There is a theological story to be told about sleep. It is about sleep as a gift, and not an affliction, despite the unfortunate occasional conflation of sleep with sloth. It is a state of grace and not of sin. It refreshes and renews, yet can never be earned; all we can do is to be in a posture of receptivity so that it falls upon us. Sleep is profoundly precarious and sometimes frustratingly elusive and is suggestive of the fragility and vulnerability of human existence. Good sleep is a prerequisite to a good waking life. The eschatological character of sleep points us to reflect on mortality and resurrection.

Is it possible to speak of a 'theology of sleep'? I argue that it is possible but that it is not to be found as a coherent body of teaching or theological exploration. Rather, a theology of sleep is found articulated in Christian practices such as the Office of Compline, the keeping of vigils and the Examen of Consciousness, and in evening hymnody and prayers before bed. I will suggest that the word *theosomnia*, which I will define more fully below, encapsulates this understanding of sleep.

Sleep within different disciplines

Many, if not all, books on the subject of sleep begin by pointing out that human beings sleep for approximately one third of their lives. That is perfectly true. There are also times and stages of life, for example in infancy and teenage years, when sleep occupies somewhat more than a third of life; at other times, somewhat less – for example, in old age when sleep is more elusive. Either way sleep is a significant aspect of human experience. That third of one's life is generative and sustaining in a way that is often underestimated, not least in the context of an increasingly frenetic, unceasing 24/7 society.

For a long time, sleep has been regarded as a foreign land that is only glimpsed in dreams or notable when unconsolidated or disordered. It is a land that is at the same time familiar (we go there every night) and yet deeply strange (what is going on in my mind and body when I sleep?). Sleep has been a subject of literature and philosophy for millennia, at least as far back as Aristotle, and latterly modern scientific curiosity has extended to it. Advances in neuro-science have contributed to this, as have the insights of evolutionary biologists. The science of sleep is becoming more sophisticated, even if experience of sleep itself remains as strange as ever.

Despite intensive research, science in its broadest sense has not yet reached a consensus on the origins and purposes of sleep. When we are asleep, the brain is as active as when we are awake, if not more so: the brain does not rest, even if the body does. In terms of evolutionary biology, the question is why animals in general and humans in particular sleep for so long when they are profoundly vulnerable to attack by wild animals or other humans whilst asleep. That question aside, others have asked what the significance of sleep might be philosophically, sociologically, psychologically and, now, theologically.

Disciplines in the human sciences have also begun to engage with sleep as a phenomenon that has an impact beyond the simple fact of doing it. Sociologists such as Simon Williams see sleep as a way of exploring how human bodies interact with the world and how it 'sheds important light on their social lives, social roles and social relationships'.[1] Sleep tells us about our bodies and that our being-in-the-world is 'irreducibly embodied'. This importantly directs attention to the cost of poor sleep, not least in a society in which sleep is pressurised, squeezed and sometimes seen as a luxury or sign of weakness.

---

1   Williams, S.J. (2005) Sleep and Society: Sociological Adventures into the (Un)known. Abingdon: Routledge, p.4.

There is also wide and keen interest in what constitutes good sleep or the pursuit of better sleep. This interest is reflected in the growing interest in, and prevalence of, articles in lifestyle magazines and on websites. Sleep as a source of rest is seen as part of an enduring interest in wellbeing, in its widest sense; a holistic appreciation of what it means to be a complete human being: body, mind and spirit. Rest and repose, which are close cousins of sleep, although they can be mutually exclusive, are part of the generative character of sleep. Psychology, for example, is interested in the relationship between sleep and mental health, or more precisely poor sleep and mental health, asking if poor sleep leads to poor mental health or vice versa.

Can there be a 'theology of sleep'?

And this is what theology can bring in its account of sleep. This is the uniqueness of the theological discipline, one that draws a community of faith to worship and from that to seek out and serve the coming Kingdom of God in the world. My touchstone of the merits or possibility of a theology of sleep is in the way it prompts a doxological response: does it issue in praise and thanksgiving?

If there is such a thing as a theology of sleep, then where is it to be found? My conviction is that a very rich operating theology of sleep is to be found in ecclesially based, but not ecclesiastically controlled, pastoral and liturgical practice; that is to say, we find it in prayers, hymnody and liturgical seasons. This 'working theology' of sleep, that the vast majority of Christians encounter, is found in what we sing and pray and how we counsel. Moreover, it does that in the prosaic actions of the beginning and end of the day which are integral to the hallowing of every moment. This is where the theology of sleep, rooted in biblical narrative and metaphor, is found and practised. Sleep is also a part of mystical theology in that it cherishes sleep as a gift from God as an act of faith and hope because it entrusts that which is outside our conscious life experience to the watchfulness of the Other, to God.

We have seen that a range of disciplines engage with the phenomenon of sleep, going beyond formal academic disciplines into lifestyle magazines, websites and broadcasting. Sleep is not generally treated by theology in a systematic way. This seems a strange and unfortunate oversight, yet one this book seeks to redress. To do this we will explore sleep and theology by touching on doctrine, pastoral theology, ethics, eschatology worship, contemplative writing and theological anthropology.

Christian theology has a story to tell about sleep, drawing both from its texts and its practices. Whilst theology is not totally silent on sleep, it is not surprising that it is not well accounted for, partly because it is not possible, as we shall see, to state that there is a sole 'biblical understanding' of what sleep is or what its merits or demerits are so far as scripture is concerned: it is much more diffuse than that. Christian practices such as prayers before bed, the Office of Night Prayer (also known as Compline) and evening hymnody also use a broad spectrum of images around sleeping (and its corollary waking) that add to the different locations which need situating on the map of the theological themes of sleep.

The theological themes are not remote from lived Christian experience. A systematic theology of sleep can enable Christian disciples both to become more aware of the nature of their sleep in terms of health and wellbeing, and to deepen and enrich the practices of their lived faith. It is perhaps no accident that in the absence of a systematic theology of sleep over the centuries we can look to prayer and hymnody as a source of reflection. The instinctive sense of Christian believers and communities is that sleeping and waking are profoundly important and should be. Indeed, the practices around sleep are themselves inter-generational and draw in an oftentimes-overlooked constituency in the Church, children; for example, in the act of praying with children before bed or singing lullabies.

It is not my purpose in what follows to suggest in any way that the practices around sleep are erroneous or misguided, but rather to say that they can be further informed by a more systematic approach. This approach will highlight some of the contradictions in the 'biblical account' of sleep (if we think there must be a sole consistent theology of sleep in the variety of texts that make up Holy Scripture). The contradictions serve to enrich the different ways in which sleep can be understood as theologically significant.

There is a prior question before we continue, and that is to ask: is it really possible to theologise about sleep? I bring to this study the fundamental conviction that theology must be able to address all aspects of our lives because theology most properly is not simply the study of the bolt-on bits of life, but is all encompassing. Rather, theology is intentional reflection upon the operation of God in the lives of creatures and the natural world. Mike Higton asks if there can be a theology of anything.[2] In asking this, his preliminary concern is about theological method: this helps us approach sleep theologically. Following Higton's method, two questions must be addressed. Does sleep stand out as a salient phenomenon when the world is explored theologically? Does it merit theological attention? This book is predicated on the answer being 'yes' to both questions. First, sleep is a human, and indeed animal, phenomenon. There are many other areas of human experience, food and sex to name but two, that occupy substantially less time of a human life when compared with sleep and that are the subject of exhaustive theological and ethical reflection. Second, it merits theological attention because fundamentally, as Higton suggests, a theology of *anything* must allow for the inherent goodness of the subject in question and that the pursuit of theology rests in the God who is love. It is also demonstrably the case that the biblical witness sees the sleeping body as an arena of divine activity. I hope this will be seen throughout this book.

Nick Jowett has suggested that 'in a time of declining resources in both Church and society, the pressure to overwork is driven by competitiveness and guilt, but the results of forcing ourselves on against nature are likely to be diminishing. It is time that we took more seriously a positive theology of sleep.'[3] As a priest and pastoral theologian, I am very aware that theology is grounded in and enriched by ecclesially rooted pastoral practice. That awareness should not, however, prompt a crass attempt to *apply* theological insight to everyday situations or to create a therapeutic theology of sleep. That sort of approach would imply a transaction between prayer-informed reasoning and a 'practical' outcome which would turn theology into a solutions-based technique, rather than the opening up of an expansive reflection on God's world and creatures.

---

2   Higton, M. 'A Theology of the University.' Paper given at the Society for the Study of Theology. http://www.theologysociety.org.uk/Higton.pdf, accessed 4 April 2013.

3   Jowett, N. (2013) 'A Theology of Slumber.' *Church Times.* http://www.churchtimes. co.uk/articles/2014/14-february/comment/opinion/a-theology-of-slumber, accessed 5 August 2015.

In *A Theology of Everyday Life*, Karl Rahner asks, 'Is there such a thing as a theology of sleeping?' Answering his own question he says that 'most certainly there is'.[4] The reasons Rahner gives include: a scriptural basis, which reflects a broad spectrum of attitudes towards sleep; and the way in which the biblical witness connects with sleep, 'as an image and reflection of a deeper reality of human existence', primarily because of the connections between sleep and mortality. Rahner also sees the 'inner relaxation' of sleep that opens a person to dreams. The issues raised above, in terms of consciousness, will, memory and self, are also features of sleep that are worthy of a 'theology'. Sleep, for Rahner, is 'peaceful and relaxed, a communication with the depth in which needs to be grounded and rooted whatever makes us free as human beings, all conscious spanning of life, if we want to remain whole or wish to be'.

The image and likeness of God

A foundational theological supposition is that each person is precious in the sight of God and that part of the character of being human is that life is and can be received as a sheer gift. The nature of the giftedness of life is that none of us has earned the right to have been born or has strenuously worked at being born in the first place. This is our character of being creatures: beings that derive their origin from outside themselves, and that origin is God. The very creation has giftedness embedded into it from the beginning through God's creative action. If we are able to acknowledge that, then when we consider sleep we see that it too has the character of gift.

Throughout history a human problem has been that we are not good at receiving gifts, or we are suspicious of them simply because they *are* gifts, unmerited and grace-filled. The early heresy of Pelagianism can be characterised in this way. It took the view that human beings had to work for salvation and thereby undermined the graced nature of human life in relation to God. The *gift* of sleep subverts that approach and thus speaks of grace. Indeed, the more

---

4   Rahner, K. (2010) *A Theology of Everyday Life*, trans. and ed. A.S. Kidder. Maryknoll: Orbis, p.183.

one works to fall asleep the less likely, often, it is to come. Sleep has rather to be received as the gift it is.

Another tendency is to reject the giftedness of creation and to assume that there is an underlying hostility in God's purposes to that which is good and is a gift. This may broadly be characterised as a Calvinist approach which sees nature in general, and human nature in particular, as essentially corrupted, not just marred and despoiled through human sin as a later act. In this account sleep is not plausible as a gift but rather a burden or a snare which can trap the earnest, hardworking believer. This is the approach that sees sleep as equating to sloth.

This leads us to see that sleep highlights the essential connection between the body and the spirit that must be made in being human. This is about human identity and valuing the embodied character of being human. Sleep enables us to reject a dualism that somehow denigrates the body, because sleep is a profoundly embodied act. Whilst sleeping we cannot in any way give an account of what our mind is doing, or the nature of our consciousness and rationality. This was something about which Augustine of Hippo (354–430) writes in *Confessions*. Rationality subsides when we sleep, and if being a rational creature is what defines me over and above animals, what does that make me when I sleep?

That particular question will be left hanging until Chapter 1, but asking that question in relation to sleep also reminds us of something that should not need stating but sometimes does: we are not machines. This is stating the obvious, but much discourse around being human tends to assume that sleep is akin to the shutting down of the computer that is the brain, or the hardware that is the body. In another sphere neuroscientists are becoming far more aware that, rather than equate the brain to a computer, much more will be gained in asking how computers can replicate the human brain, the most complex organism in the cosmos. My own laptop offers me three choices when I click on power: restart, shut down and sleep. But the brain, and being human, is very much more intricate than that and has a plasticity that no computer can possibly replicate.

These then are the key markers in the divine–human relationship on which we can begin to build and explore sleep and theology, such that we can develop a Christian theology of sleep.

Sleep through the centuries

What is sleep?

Circadian neuroscientists Steven Lockley and Russell Foster state that, 'for centuries, we have regarded sleep as a simple suspension of activity, a passive state of unconsciousness, and for centuries we have been wrong'.[5] If sleep is more than a simple suspension of activity or a passive state of unconsciousness, then what positively can be said about it? Passivity aside, sleep clearly moves the body into an altered, if not passive, state of consciousness. Writing about human, and wider mammalian, sleep, James Horne lists a comprehensive set of observable features: 'a typical body posture; specific site or nest for this behaviour; physical inactivity; a regular occurrence influenced by a circadian clock; more stimulation is required to rouse the animal than during wakefulness'.[6] Other writers have suggested that

> sleep is a physiological, complex, integrated behavior characterized by a significant reduction of the response to the external stimuli, by characteristic posture, usually in a special environment, by a characteristic change in neurophysiological recordings of brain activity and by a homeostatic increase after its restriction.[7]

Again that definition combines observable behaviour and neuroscientific insight. Recourse to the brain as the definitive organ of the body by which to measure sleep is a feature of sleep research. The brain and body cannot be separated in defining sleep.

A survey of sleep literature across disciplines shows that the field that currently has the academic high ground is neuroscience. That which can be measured, especially by complex technology, is held in high regard in a broadly secular society. Furthermore, exploration of the brain seems to be the final frontier of understanding human physiology and the body. Neuroscience is the default discipline to which recourse is made in answering the question of what sleep is. Yet simply asking what sleep is leads into other disciplines and questions

---

5   Lockley, S.W. and Foster, R.G. (2012) *Sleep: A Very Short Introduction*. Oxford: Oxford University Press, p.1.

6   Horne, J. (1988) *Why We Sleep: The Functions of Sleep in Humans and Other Mammals*. Oxford: Oxford University Press, p.7.

7   Maquet, P., Smith, C., and Stickgold, R. (2003) 'Introduction' to *Sleep and Brain Plasticity*, eds P. Maquet *et al*. Oxford: Oxford University Press, p.7.

about what constitutes being human: is the brain akin to the mind or even the soul? What happens to all three during sleep? And that leads to questions about memory and reason in relation to sleep. The reason these questions arise is that sleep is a highly distinctive time when questions about who we are and the nature of what constitutes being human are reframed. So other measures of being human also feature when sleep is studied.

Neuroscience

Lockley and Foster describe sleep in terms of neuroscience and the insights that the electroencephalogram (EEG) has opened up. This showed that in normal circumstances the sleep cycle alternates between two distinct types of sleep: rapid eye movement (REM) and non-rapid eye movement (NREM). The number of cycles depends on the length of sleep: but on average there are four to five cycles per night, based on a cycle of 90–100 minutes. The EEG shows the four stages of NREM sleep as having different features. Stage one is referred to as somnolence or drowsy sleep and can feature sudden twitches and jerks of the limbs. Stage two shows on the EEG short bursts of activity called 'sleep spindles', but muscular activity tends to decrease and conscious awareness of the external environment disappears. Stages three and four are known as slow-wave sleep. REM sleep is sometimes known as 'paradoxical sleep' because its EEG patterns are almost identical to those of a fully awake individual. Even then there are different patterns of sleep: at different stages of life; times of stress; during illness; or the phenomenon of 'larks' and 'owls', more accurately termed 'diurnal preferences'.

Sleep and patterns of behaviour

So another way to ask what sleep is, is to describe its behavioural features. Lockley and Foster list six: first, it is a rapidly reversible state of immobility with greatly reduced responsiveness, the reversibility thus distinguishing it from hibernation; second, increased arousal thresholds (i.e. needing more noise to be woken) and a decreased responsiveness to external stimulation; third, posture and place preferences, for example snuggling up in a bed; fourth, behavioural rituals before sleep, for example circling, yawning and nest-making; fifth, circadian regulation and the persistence of a 24-hour rhythm under constant conditions; and finally, a behaviour that is homeostatically regulated so the lost sleep is associated with a drive and need for sleep. We see that sleep cannot be described solely in neurological or behavioural criteria.

Sleep can be described but its purpose is not wholly clear. This makes it particularly, if not uniquely, intriguing.

Philosophy

Sleep has been studied for at least 2500 years. The Greek philosopher-physicians Alcmaeon, Hippocrates and Aristotle all put forward theories on the causes and functions of sleep, and their questions and musings framed the debate about sleep for the next two millennia.

Early Greek cultural ideas around sleep were associated with the stomach and the idea that warm vapours rose from the gut during digestion to initiate sleep and that different foods could influence sleepiness. From an early Christian perspective, this early view is reflected in the writing of St Gregory of Nyssa (c.335–c.395) in *On the Making of Man*. Gregory writes about vapours and the senses:

> ...if the apparatus of the organs of sense should be closed and sleep hindered by some occupation, the nervous system, becoming filled with the vapours, is naturally and spontaneously extended so that the part which has had its density increased by the vapours is rarefied by the process of extension.[8]

On the associated subject of yawning Gregory describes the physical features of the yawn, with the point being that 'smoky denseness which had been detained in the neighbouring parts is emitted together with the exit of the breath. And often the like may happen even after sleep when any portion of those vapours remains in the region spoken of undigested and unexhaled.'

In the seventeenth century René Descartes suggested the involvement of the brain as the organ mediating sleep and wake states (which might be expected of the originator of the *Cogito*), identifying the pineal gland as significant, and rightly so, as the site of melatonin production.

---

8   Gregory of Nyssa, *On the Making of Man* (Limovia.net), 62.

The mid-twentieth century saw the great technological advance of the measurement of brain activity during sleep in the EEG, which prompted a rapid expansion in the study of sleep. At the same time, the daily rhythms of sleep and temperature in the absence of external influences had been noted and REM sleep described.

By the 1940s and 1950s researchers showed that the brainstem could greatly influence sleep and that the recording from that region changed markedly during sleep and wakefulness. Lockley and Foster note that, 'collectively, their work enabled these researchers to conclude that multiple structures within the brainstem are involved in maintaining wakefulness, and the generation of the NREM–REM cycle of sleep'. More recently a wide body of philosophical writing about sleep has developed and spilled into the social sciences.[9]

Biblical

Sonia Ancoli-Israel has shown that questions about sleep are raised in the Hebrew Scriptures and rabbinic teaching. She seeks to synthesise early Hebrew thought with modern scientific insights in terms of REM sleep and NREM sleep. Ancoli-Israel maps the four stages of NREM onto the different Hebrew terms for sleep. There is no single word in Hebrew for sleep. Rather a number of words describe different states of sleep:

> '*Tenumah*' is often used to mean 'drowsy', which could refer to dozing or light stage 1 sleep (Isaiah 5.27; Psalm 76.6). '*Yashen*' and '*shenah*' are used for conscious thought which becomes unconscious and involuntary, words that could also describe stage 2 sleep... '*Radum*' implies a heavy or deep stages 3 and 4 sleep... The last stage of sleep, '*tardemah*', also refers to a period where the flow of thoughts continue in dreams or revelation, a perfect description of REM sleep...[10]

Changing sleep patterns are also reflected in the Bible – for example, the change with ageing: 'The Hebrew word "*yashan*" that is one of the words for "sleep" also means "old".' With the attendant dangers of

---

9   For a comprehensive survey and analysis of sleep in philosophy see Morgan Wortham, S. (2013) *The Poetics of Sleep: From Aristotle to Nancy*. London: Bloomsbury.

10 Ancoli-Israel, S. (2003) 'Sleep disorders in the Bible.' *Jewish Bible Quarterly*, Vol. 31, No. 3.

anachronism, Ancoli-Israel's method starts with what is currently known of sleeping disorders and reads them back into biblical and rabbinic material.

Why do we sleep?

Whilst explanations for *how* we sleep, in terms of what is going on in the body and brain, are well advanced, why we sleep remains 'frustratingly unresolved' even to Lockley and Foster who are eminent in their field. It might seem sui generis that sleep is about rest and inactivity. Just because what the brain is doing when someone is 'asleep' can be measured does not mean we know why we sleep. There are criteria, beyond what is externally observable, to be considered. The fact that someone's eyes are shut does not mean that they are asleep; measurements by EEG would establish that. But when someone is asleep their eyes are shut, if REM sleep is not included. Shut eyes are not an indication of sleep across the animal kingdom. Some species can sleep with their eyes open. That is an extreme example perhaps of what might be called attentive or vigilant sleep. It also undermines the apparently simple observation that sleep is a time when eyes are shut. Those species do this because of heightened vulnerability during sleep. That prompts biologists to question the evolutionary purpose of sleep: why do it?

What is the impact of sleep?

The 1970s saw questions about sleep in a markedly different direction: 'do we really need sleep at all?'[11] Ray Meddis wrote that 'sleep serves no important function in modern man and that, in principle at least, man is capable of living happily without it'.[12] Meddis' contribution to what sleep is reverses the suppositions of behavioural observation – that sleep is a means of achieving vital rest after physical and mental exhaustion, to overcome fatigue or recuperate or revive. Rather, he sees it as a way to maximise the chances of survival during the long

---

11   Dement, W.C. (1972) *Some Must Watch While Some Must Sleep.* San Francisco: W.H. Freeman, p.3.

12   Meddis, R. (1977) *The Sleep Instinct.* Cited by Morgan Wortham, *The Poetics of Sleep.*

periods when there is really nothing to be done, after hunting and other basic tasks, or presumably when it is too dark to hunt or carry out those tasks. Thus sleep is a good way of killing time, and rather than being vulnerable the sleeping body is simply inconspicuous. Meddis supposed that something in the brain could be identified to effect an adjustment that would render sleep a thing of the past, a development he expected to be close at hand. Twenty years on, and with no simple sleep eradication technique available, this theme was taken up in Jonathan Coe's novel *House of Sleep*, in which a doctor who specialises in sleep disorders is in fact using his patients to see how sleep itself can be eradicated (taking as his heroine the late British Prime Minister Margaret Thatcher, who famously existed on very little sleep). The doctor eventually descends into mental illness and paranoia by his dystopian dream of negating the need for sleep.

In a nutshell, then, what sleep is and why creatures do it is not settled despite the tremendous amount of research undertaken and discoveries made. There are interesting new insights in the field of sleep biology. Lockley and Foster point to sleep as allowing for cellular restoration, energy conservation and the consolidation of memory. The impact of neglecting those factors speaks for itself. Sleep deprivation has been shown to impair cognition, memory and attention through depriving the brain of essential neural processing within the higher cortical brain. The impact of lack of sleep is considerable and conversely the benefits of sleep measurable and substantial. It is little wonder that sleep deprivation is widely recognised as torture under Article 1 of the United Nations' *Convention against Torture and Other Cruel, Inhuman or Degrading Treatment or Punishment* (1984).

Theosomnia: explorations in theology and sleep

Theosomnia

As I have sought to stress above, theology deals with lived human experience in the light of that which has been received in revelation – scriptural and in human encounter – from and with God. Sleep is worthy of such attention. The danger is that such explorations could be pursued in the abstract and esoteric. In an attempt to base this in a less abstract setting I have coined a neologism, 'theosomnia'. This seeks to capture the beautiful and mystical verse from the Song of Songs: 'I sleep, yet my heart wakes' (Song of Songs 5.2).

Theosomnia is a recognisable word as a conjunction of the two words *theos* and (*in*)*somnia*.

Theos is simply the Greek word for God. *Insomnia*, the chronic want of sleep, derives from Somnus, the god of sleep in Roman mythology. Simply, and literally, the word *theosomnia* means 'God-sleep'. By it I mean hallowed sleep: in other words, sleep that is intentionally open to God; is blessed by God; and is offered to God. Typically, this is sleep consciously committed to God, for example in Compline, other prayers before bed or a prayerful awareness of God's presence, 'both waking and sleeping', or through a spiritual exercise such as the Examen of Consciousness. *Theosomnia* extends to the cessation of sleep through waking expectantly, and includes the possibility of dreams as having the capacity to reorient the day.

Theosomnia is the sleep of the disciple drawn from the sleep seen in Jesus as he slept in the boat on the Sea of Galilee during the storm (Mark 4.35–41 and parallels). This is sleep of radical openness to the Father, since it is a Christological posture. *Theosomnia* acknowledges that sleep is a time when God can work deep within the self, when control is lost and the ego, like the storm, is stilled: 'He must increase, but I must decrease' (John 3.30).

Sleep – 'An half adieu unto the world'

As we begin the task of this book – exploring theology and sleep – we first have to excavate the foundations of the notion of *theosomnia* so that it is not an abstraction but a lived engagement with the presence of the living God: to do that we will first turn our attention to the work of Sir Thomas Browne (1605–1682). Browne was a noted polymath and churchman and, in his *Religio Medici* (1643), wrote a meditation on sleep that has an autobiographical and confessional sense to it.[13] The fact that Browne reflects on sleep in prayer illustrates the point that sleep is well articulated in Christian understanding in

---

13   Browne, T., ed. Winney, J, (1963) *Religio Medici*. Cambridge: Cambridge University Press.

prayer, liturgy and hymnody which, along with the Bible, are the source material for a systematic theology of sleep.

Browne's prayer, as we shall see, is an example of a non-systematic theology of sleep that is expressed doxologically: doctrinal and biblical references woven into prayer. It entrusts him to sleep, mindful of its pitfalls and dangers. Throughout it he references scripture and his human experience and says of sleep that it is 'the dormative I take to bedward' and continues: 'I need no other laudnam than [prayer] to make me sleep.' Browne, whom we can now call a *theosomniac*, writes that, on going to bed, 'truly' tis a fit time for devotion; and therefore I cannot lay my head without an orison, and take my farewell in a colloquy with God'.

That captures the impulse to see the boundary between being awake and being asleep as a hallowed time and a time, as Browne puts it, 'after which I close mine eyes in security, content to take my leave of the sun and sleep unto the Resurrection'. Praying before sleep, in the expectation of waking in the morning, is what Browne calls 'an half adieu unto the world'. Sleep is the 'moderating point between life and death', yet in life and in death, the Christian conviction is whilst we sleep, in life or death, the believer's heart wakes to God.

Browne references many of the themes that will be explored in greater depth in subsequent chapters.[14] His meditation maps out the terrain of this book and the doctrinal markers with which we will engage. A brief analysis of the prayer will serve as an introduction to our exploration in two ways. First, there are biblical references to which he is directly alluding. This is not an exhaustive list of biblical references to sleep, but is a good starter. Second, Browne raises some fundamental theological themes: sin, seeing sleep as possibly a consequence of humanity's fallen state; watchfulness; the abandon and vulnerability of the sleeping individual; sleep as a regenerative state, both physically and spiritually; sleep and mortality; and the sense that this worldly human condition exists in 'drowsy days'.

In a rich set of images Browne's prayer exposes contradictions and paradoxes in how sleep is treated in the Bible. Importantly though, he sets sleep within a doctrine of creation. The opening lines locate sleep in the creative act of God who calls light into being – 'Let there

---

14 Browne, *Religio Medici.*

be light' (Genesis 1.3) – and frames it by day and night: '*The night is come, like to the day, / depart not Thou, great GOD, away.*' There is an allusion to Christ, the Light of the World, the one who shines in the darkness, and that the darkness has not overcome (John 1.5). Given that sleep is predominantly a darkness-based activity, it could be an opportunity to collude with the darkness, and recognising this, Browne asks that his own sinfulness does not '*Eclipse the lustre of Thy light*'.

Darkness alludes to sinfulness in Scripture. It contrasts the children of the darkness with the children of the day. A more lasting concern of traditional Christian approaches to the night and sleep are less about sins of commission and rather more sins of omission. Sleep represents a time of loss of control represented in the possibility that '*dreams my head infest*'. Loss of personal control raises the question of who is in control of the sleeper. Traditionally the most likely suspect is Satan: prayers that ask for protection from 'nightly fears and fantasies' usually have Satan in mind, or, as Browne puts it, '*guard me 'gainst those watchful foes, whose eyes are open while mine close*'. The sense of menace is clear.

It is not that sleep is sinful per se, rather that the opportunity for sin comes through, for example, erotic dreams or sloth in the form of a surfeit of sleep. This is mitigated by the way in which sleep is prepared for. Compline opens with confession as the fall of darkness heightens the acute awareness of sin and failings throughout the past day that can be carried into the long, dark night. Browne prays that the lustrous light of God is not eclipsed by '*my sins, black as the night*'.

Compline prepares the Christian for the profound vulnerability and abandon of sleep (the state that the evolutionary biologists cannot comprehend). Weaving together both the sense of vulnerability and God's watchfulness, Browne pleads, '*Thou whose nature cannot sleep, / on my temples sentry keep.*' In that Browne is clearly alluding to the death of Sisera at the hands of Jael who took a hammer and drove a tent peg through his temple because 'he was lying fast asleep from weariness' (Judges 4.21).

The theological assertion of the watchfulness of God – '*Thou whose nature cannot sleep*' – derives from Psalm 127, 'The Lord who watches over Israel shall neither slumber nor sleep', yet equally Psalm 44 implies that God really can sleep: 'Up, Lord, why sleepest thou, wilt thou be absent from us forever' (Psalm 44.23). Elsewhere God is described as being aroused from sleep (78.65). Nevertheless, the conviction that God watches over the sleeper is enduringly significant. It assumes a relationship between the Creator and the creature: '*keep still in my horizon; for to me the sun makes not the day, but Thee*'. There is a sense that the watcher and the watched over have a mutual eye on each other.

Keeping watchful is not simply what God 'does' when a person sleeps. The believer is called to keep watch too. Sleep, as already noted, is represented both as a time of inattention and deep attention to God. Attentive sleep is primarily shown by Browne in sleep open to the possibility of dreams: '*make my sleep a holy trance, that I may, my rest being wrought, awake into some holy thought*'. Some of the literature about dreams is highly speculative and perhaps over-imaginative – and it is not the purpose of this book to analyse dreams – nevertheless it would be counter to biblical witness and human experience to dismiss the impact and power of dreams.

It is not unknown that dreams, or at the very least the act of 'sleeping on it', can influence a decision or course of action, not unlike Joseph who woke and arose from sleep and led Mary and Jesus to safety in Egypt, having been warned in a dream of Herod's intentions (Matthew 2.13). In that regard sleep can be the arena for theophany, a manifestation of the divine presence. Sleep is integral to the relationship between mortals and God in God's self-communication in dreams and nocturnal revelation. That in itself is an ambiguous experience, such as Jacob experienced at Bethel (Genesis 28.10–22): '*Let no dreams my head infest, but such as Jacob's temples blest.*' We can note that not all dreams are benign or decisive in the Bible. For example, the dreams of Saul are very unsettling and his sleep disturbed as a consequence.

Sleep can be a fearful time, especially when elusive or disturbed. There is a deeper, perhaps connected, fear, which is often articulated with regard to the relationship between sleep and mortality. The notion of loss of control connects sleep with death, when all is relinquished at a time when not even dreams will happen, because sleep anticipates death: '*sleep is a death; O make me try, / by sleeping, what it is to die; / and as gently lay my head / on my grave, as now my bed*'. What if, like

Sisera, I never wake again: am I prepared? Sleep also relates to the fear of a 'sudden death' because it means dying unprepared.

Alongside the positive imagery of light, these fears of darkness, night, sleep and associations with death give the context to liturgical practices such as the Lucinarium and traditional prayers before bed, both for children and adults. The anticipation of death is also, for the Christian disciple, the anticipation of resurrection: '*however I rest, great GOD, let me / awake again at last with Thee; / and thus assur'd, behold I lie / securely, or to awake or die*'. In the reference to waking again, Browne refers directly to sleep and the resurrection and the Christian hope that the believer will be awakened on the Last Day.

Browne speaks of a time when he will '*never / Sleep again but wake for ever*'. That reference alerts us to the eschatological dimension of sleep and the nature of time. The eschatological parables of the Kingdom often have the refrain 'stay awake', as does the account of Gethsemane, and sleep is an integral feature. For example, both the attentive and inattentive character of sleep is deployed as a motif in the case of the sleeping bridesmaids who miss the arrival of the bridegroom, with all its messianic overtones (Matthew 25.1–13).

When exploring sleep it is easy to focus upon the physical act of falling asleep, the phases of sleep and what sleep signifies and represents. However, a theology of sleep is incomplete without the flipside of the wakeful life of the day or at the very least how one wakes, and how sleep has prepared for that. For Christian theology, if sleeping speaks of death and mortality, then waking says resurrection. Again Browne captures this: '*These are my drowsie days; in vain / I do not wake to sleep again: / O come that hour, when I shall never / sleep again, but wake for ever.*' The *theosomniac* has to be mindful of waking as well as sleeping, since sleep delivers waking, and vice versa – a virtuous circle. In other words, the *theosomniac* does not simply focus on sleep, but rejoices in the day as a gift which then makes sense of the entrusting of the self to sleep.

Sinking deeper

Having introduced the key concepts around sleep and theology, including *theosomnia*, I hope to have given a plausible case for the value of a theology of sleep that is engaging theologically, interesting intellectually, and nourishing spiritually and in the life of a Christian disciple. We have seen through Thomas Browne an example of a sustained meditation on sleep that draws in many and various strands. These strands will be developed in the remainder of the book.

The first chapter considers how, theologically, we prepare for sleep. This begins with prayer. It goes on to look at some of the parallels between prayer and sleep as we examine the role of posture in both using the work of the French philosopher Jean-Luc Nancy. Using the lullaby as a musical and communicative form that is a prelude to sleep, this chapter will explore childhood prayers, Compline and evening hymns.

Chapter 1 also reflects on issues around identity and personhood in sleep. Prompted by Augustine's reflection on sleep in his *Confessions*, we ask 'When am I most me? When I am awake or when I am asleep?', and 'What does the apparent suspension of time and distortion of rationality do to my relationship with God and with myself?' One way into those questions is through thinking more about adoration in *theosomnia* as we use the writings of Thérèse of Lisieux on sleep, contemplation and mysticism. Drawing on contemplatives of earlier centuries, we explore further the leitmotif given by the Song of Songs, 'I sleep yet my heart wakes' (Song of Songs 5.2).

In Chapter 2, we explore the further themes of vigilance and watchfulness using the motif of the sentinel and how it is treated in the Old and New Testaments and informs some of the parables of Jesus. This is taken to extreme lengths described by St Bede in his *Life of St Cuthbert*, who denies himself sleep for prolonged periods. This raises the question of the way in which a gift from God like sleep, or food, can be self-denied in practices akin to fasting, and to what end.

In exploring the waking life in relation to sleep, Chapter 3 opens up sleep in relation to resurrection, time and eschatology. It uncovers how language about sleep, in scripture and Christian usage, is not used as a euphemism to deny the reality of death but rather an image that draws from a rich understanding of the Christian hope and the life of the world to come. That prompts reflection on how the Christian should wake as well as prepare for sleep.

In drawing together the themes of the book the Conclusion will offer a theological anthropology of sleep in which a wide understanding of *theosomnia* enriches human experience in relation to God, the self and other people. In so doing connections will be made with pastoral theology in the way in which language around sleep and death is understood and articulated as well as the connections with pastoral care surrounding mental health, wellbeing and bereavement.

It is clear that sleep is integral to the embodied life of each person, at all stages of life, and it feeds the body and the mind. The increased interest in sleep in contemporary society has not been reflected in sustained theological engagement with it, but my hope is that this book will change that direction. Mining the notion of *theosomnia* will reveal many jewels of Christian theological wisdom and practices that have lain hidden, unacknowledged or underappreciated for too long, and it may encourage others to explore further and reappraise how they might be called to be *theosomniacs* themselves.

1

INTO YOUR HANDS, O LORD, I COMMEND MY SPIRIT

The mystery of sleep

There is a moment when I am no longer awake but I am asleep. Whilst falling asleep is familiar to everyone it is still a deeply strange experience and hard to account for. The body and mind enter a new mode of existence but regular bodily activity continues: when sleeping we still breathe, our hearts beat and our brains work. On the whole, we are aware of impending sleep, but cannot account for the moment it comes upon us. By definition, if I am asleep then I cannot give an account of what is happening to me. I can only give such an account if I am awake, and I can only be aware of what happens to me if I am awake. This is a mystery. Dreams are but one expression of this mystery and feature in Biblical and other spiritual material.

In Christian practice the Office of Compline maps out the onset of sleep. It is an intentional practice of approaching the mystery of sleep and does so in a spiritually practical way. The spiritual postures encouraged by Compline are penitence, trust, awareness of mortality and hope of resurrection. At its heart is the refrain, 'into your hands O Lord, I commend my spirit'. That very phrase is uttered by Jesus on the cross and its use in Compline signals a sense of surrender into the will of God, which is most supremely evident in the death of Jesus, and which is echoed in lying down to sleep.

The way in which this gift can be received takes us to the heart of what theosomnia, hallowed sleep committed to God, is. This is an act of body and spirit together, indeed it illustrates that body and spirit are inseparable. In this the self is called to relinquish control of the ego and the activity of the waking life. There is continuity between the waking and sleeping self, but it is also qualitatively different. This posture is one of vulnerability, in many ways, both spiritual and physical. The adoption of a physical posture for sleep invites exploration of a theological posture.

The onset of sleep: posture of body and spirit

The mind and body

The onset of sleep is something that can be welcomed or it can be resisted, depending on the situation, or indeed it can be elusive and frustrating. Linguistically we speak of falling asleep or going to sleep. The phrase 'going to sleep' suggests that there is a dynamic transition from one state to another. Sleep prompts a qualitative change of being: in going to sleep I move from the wakeful state to the sleeping state. That is potentially unsettling in terms of self-identity. The phrase 'falling asleep' implies either that something falls upon the person or that the person falls into a state from which they must rise.[1]

Either way – *falling* or *going to* – the onset of sleep is essentially passive in that it cannot be manufactured. It is a release, a letting go of wakefulness. It is a phenomenon that reminds us of the giftedness of life and the human inability to control or will every aspect of life. The neuroscientist Iain McGilchrist suggests that 'some things, like sleep, simply cannot be willed'.[2] Natural sleep, that is, sleep not induced by medication, injury or some other means, can only happen when the conditions are right.

To consider sleep is to consider how control over oneself, mind and body, has its limits. The action of going to sleep or falling asleep has to be invited but cannot be made to happen, as many insomniacs will readily testify. This demands a new way of construing human control over bodily phenomena, and also has a spiritual dimension. When we desire to go to sleep we instinctively understand that this is not something that can be willed, since that brings frustration and not the gift we seek. Sleep has to be invited. Conversely the onset of sleep at certain times can be uninvited and dangerous, for example

---

1   See the discussion in, Nancy, J-L. (2009) *The Fall of Sleep*. Translated by Charlotte Mandell. New York: Fordham University Press.

2   McGilchrist, I. (2010) *The Master and his Emissary: The Divided Brain and the Making of the Western World*. New Haven and London: Yale University Press. 180.

whilst driving or operating machinery. The ability to sleep in different circumstances, situations and stages of life varies greatly. Many adults would not find the conditions in which a six month old baby can go to sleep at all conducive. Light, noise, anxiety and physical posture can all affect the ability to sleep.

The French phenomenologist, Maurice Merleau-Ponty (1908–1961), notes that sleep is something that cannot, in normal circumstances, be manufactured; it has to be received. In that sense, and contrary to biological insights regarding circadian rhythms and melatonin levels that help dictate sleep, sleep is something external to our experience. It is something that visits us, he says, 'I call up the visitation of sleep by imitating the breathing and posture of the sleeper'. And like receiving any visitor the host must be prepared. In the case of sleep this demands a posture of receptivity:

> I lie down in bed, on my left side, with my knees drawn up; I close my eyes and breathe slowly, putting my plans out of my mind. But the power of my consciousness or will stops there'. [3]

The posture of receiving sleep is not just a physical one. This is why we find the adoption of a spiritual posture in Christian practices before sleep.

Compline: a spiritual posture

The mystery of sleep is theologically generative. Compline acknowledges sleep to be a daily turning point: it is an ending but also signals the possibilities of new beginnings. Each time we sleep we do, in some way, die to the day that has now passed and we anticipate waking to the possibilities of a new day. At that time we contemplate the giftedness of life, and the ways in which that gift is both inhabited and abused. Recollection, which is an integral feature of Compline, opens up the theological themes of grace, gratitude, reconciliation, mortality and expectation.

A brief description of Compline reveals these themes. This is not simply the analysis of the text of Compline: the timing and context both matter too. In monastic practice Compline is assumed to be

---

3   Merleau-Ponty, M. (1992) *Phenomenology of Perception*. London: Routledge. 189.

the last time of corporate prayer for the community, and signals the beginning of the greater silence. Typically monks would cover their heads with their cowls at the end of Compline as a sign that words are not to be spoken or heard. This is the aspiration of retreat groups, services of Compline or individuals at home. All should disperse in silence and make their way straight to bed. The opening words herald this, 'The Lord almighty grant us a quiet night and a perfect end'. Then there is a time of silent recollection as the past day is reviewed which leads into confession. A hymn is sung and Psalms are said. As shall be seen below the hymn and psalmody is replete with reflection on the character of sleep within the life of the Christian disciple. The fixed allocation of the psalmody enabled the Psalms to be recited by heart, on the assumption that Compline is said in at least the half-light. As it is a minor office the candles on the altar would not be lit. Likewise the brevity of the reading originally meant it could be proclaimed in the darkness from memory, and scriptural indigestion would not follow. The responsory consolidates the themes that have already been unfolded, and the gospel canticle, the Nunc Dimittis, the Song of Simeon, which follows immediately afterwards, has an end of life, end of day character, speaking as it does of departure and a greater light that is now manifest. It echoes Abbot Suger's gradation of light and its progression from the ordinary *lux* all around us, which begins to fade as night falls, that gives way to the *lumen* of Christ, which through the working of the Holy Spirit prompts the *illuminatio* of the soul. The office concludes with prayer, and all leave silently to bed.

This description of Compline is the description of a theosomniac practice. It is a hallowing of the time of sleep to God, and is mindful of and realistic about the preparation for sleep that is bigger than oneself. It also is expectant about the coming of the new day as a gift.

Grace and the disciplining of sleep

In theological terms that something is a gift associates it with God, whose entire character is one of gift. The sheer gratuity of God is captured in this understanding of God: God's giving of Godself. Sleep is graced because it is a gift, a gift with the capacity to re-create, refresh and renew. Deprivation or denial of sleep, whether imposed externally or generated physiologically is always an affliction. Sleep itself is not an affliction, despite being treated with suspicion in some theological circles which confuse sleep with sloth, which itself confuses grace with indulgence.

The sociologist Simon Williams identifies a key issue when it comes to grace suggesting that the, 'material and moral issues and associations…which converge and coalesce around the disciplines of the body in one way or another are a sign or source of both secular and spiritual salvation'.[4] He suggests this is captured and conveyed by the proverb promoted by Benjamin Franklin, and, in slightly different earlier form by Aristotle, 'Early to bed, early to rise, makes a man healthy, wealthy and wise'. There are theological traces here. Franklin's dictum implies the Protestant work ethic, something that is suspicious of sleep and wants to curtail it as much as possible. Indeed Weber, who identified this trait, says that hard work and unrelenting physical and mental toil were sure proof of genuine faith and spiritual salvation. He has an ally in William Law, who in *A Serious Call to a Devout and Holy Life* writes about 'those who waste their time in sleep'. Indeed the Book of Proverbs invites the seeker after wisdom to 'go to the ant' (Proverbs 6.6–11). Proverbs contrasts the industry and foresight of the ants with the 'lazybones' who will not rise from sleep, and concludes, 'a little sleep, a little slumber, a little folding of the hands to rest, and poverty will come upon you like a robber'. That feeds into the 'possessive individualism' which has created a culture dedicated to hard work, bodily asceticism and the transformation of the human environment. Attitudes towards sleep were a feature of early capitalism, no doubt informed by a particular reading of the Bible, and perceived in a highly negative way, 'even more sleep than is necessary…six to eight hours, is worthy of absolute moral condemnation'.[5] In contemporary political rhetoric sleep helps identify 'workers or shirkers': 'go to the ant'.

So the graced nature of sleep is not uncontested. Recourse to a key text in the Psalms is timely, 'It is in vain that you rise up early and go late to rest, eating the bread of anxious toil; for he gives sleep to his beloved' (Psalm 127.3). It seems pretty emphatic: sleep is a gift.

---

4   Williams, S.J. (2011) *The Politics of Sleep: Governing (Un)consciousness in the Late Modern Age.* Basingstoke: Palgrave Macmillan. 27.

5   Williams, *The Politics of Sleep*, 27, citing Weber, M. (1974/1930) The Protestant Ethic and the Spirit of Capitalism, trans. Parsons, T. London: Unwin.

Arnold Anderson explores the Hebrew text of the verse which can also be rendered, 'is it not in the hours of sleep that [the Lord] blesses the men he loves?' and '[The Lord] gives his beloved a reward in sleep'.[6] In any exegesis of the verse the message is clear, human labour is blessed by sleep which is God's gift.

Grace, by definition cannot be earned. Sleep, like grace, cannot be willed but can only be received as a gift. This is all the more acutely demonstrated when someone is deprived of the gift, through the torture of sleep deprivation (something St Paul recounts in 2 Corinthians), through parenthood, anxiety and such like, because it severely diminishes the potential for flourishing. When someone is sleeping well and regularly then there are measurable health and wellbeing outcomes. How else to receive grace other than with gratitude as well as penitence?

Such a grace-aware approach enriches how we prepare for sleep and how we understand it. Karl Rahner picks up on this theme in his *Theology of Everyday Life*:

> if one approached sleep…not as a merely dull succumbing to physiological mechanisms but as an agreeable and trusting acceptance of an utterly human act, then falling asleep could be seen as relating to the inner structure of prayer, which is equally a letting-go, an entrusting of one's own inner conviction to the providence of God which one lovingly accepts.[7]

This 'agreeable trusting' is an act of faith: as the evening hymn asks, 'that I may fear the grave as little as my bed'. However, preparation for sleep can involve fear. Anxiety and mental distress such as depression is not conducive to sleep and neither is fear or bereavement. There is a sense of abandonment in sleep: does God sleep? It is suggested in Psalm 44, as we have seen above. The dominant theological conviction is that 'the Lord who watches over Israel will neither slumber nor sleep' (Psalm 127.4). This is the loving acceptance of the One who never sleeps.

Dietrich Bonhoeffer sees the value in the practice of prayer before bed asking, 'when can we have any deeper sense of God's power and

---

6   Anderson, A.A. (1972) *The Book of Psalms: Volume 2*. Grand Rapids MI: Eerdmans. 867–8.

7   Rahner, *A Theology of Everyday Life*, 183.

working than in the hour when our hands lay down their work and we commit ourselves to the hands of God?'[8] It is a moment when the believer commends into God's hands, 'our unfulfilled hopes and uncompleted tasks'.[9]

Preparing for sleep and accepting the moment of sleep is an act of commitment and trust. It is what prompts Father Brown, G K Chesterton's fictional priest-detective, to remark that, 'every man who sleeps believes in God...for it is an act of faith'.[10] This is a possible response to the mystery of sleep. Whether we go to sleep or fall asleep it is a liminal place, a threshold from one way of understanding ourselves into another.

Accepting the uncertainty of the transition from waking to sleeping is a necessary prerequisite for sleep. The Christian theological response to that uncertainty sees it as a moment for faith and, as articulated in Compline, flowing into features of the Christian life such as confession, reconciliation and protection.

In many ways sleep is about completion, the completion of the waking day that is past. And yet it also places us on the threshold of waking. In terms of creation sleep is the first thing that we do in the day and not the last, 'And there was evening and there was morning the first day' (Genesis 1.5). As reflected in Jewish practice, and with traces in some Christian practice, the day begins in the evening as darkness falls rather than at sunrise. This implies that sleep is the first thing we do in the rhythm of our lives and not the last. The creative action of God over the first human, Adam, in creating his companion, is born out of a 'deep sleep' placed upon the man. That act is also an expression of humanity complete, reconciled and at one with God and each other (at least at that stage), such that human beings can sleep safely and easily in God's presence.

Recollection and confession before sleep

The day that closes is to be reviewed and considered and prompts a time of recollection and confession. The purpose of this is to recall

8   Bonhoeffer, D. (1954) *Life Together*, trans. Doberstein, J.W. London: SCM Press. 55.
9   Common Worship: *Daily Prayer*, 196.
10   Chesterton, G.K. (2003) *Father Brown: Selected Stories*. London: Collector's Library. 122.

the features of the day, to detect in it the movements of God's grace, to be reconciled to God and neighbour such that the recitation of the verse 'I will lie down in peace, for you alone Lord make me dwell in safety' can be inhabited.

John Baillie suggests that, 'every man who calls himself a Christian should go to sleep thinking about the love of God as it has visited us in the Person of His Son, Jesus Christ our Lord'.[11] Later he says, 'And in bed at night, before sleep overtakes us, or when sleep deserts us, what a profusion of thoughts compete with each other in our minds, what a kaleidoscope of images crowd in upon us, reflecting all the complexities of our daily life!' At that point thoughts vie with sleep almost in an attempt to sustain consciousness and ego into the sleeping zone.

Baillie's impulse is right, but is better informed by the notion of recollection captured by the *Examen of Consciousness* that St Ignatius Loyola describes in the *Spiritual Exercises*. Ignatius gives a framework for recollection that is less about thought and more about surrendering oneself to the onset of sleep and the completion of the day.

The *Examen* is in effect the shape and structure to a prayerful close to the day (or indeed stage of the day). Michael Ivens SJ comments that, 'the integration of the whole day into the *Exercises* includes the integration of the exercitant's last thoughts before sleep, and their thoughts on waking'. In his reflections on the *Examen*, James Martin SJ notes that the beginning of the *Examen* is to be aware of being in God's presence. From this awareness of God's presence, which is particularly pertinent at night and before the onset of sleep, five keys steps flow:

1. *Gratitude:* Recall anything from the day for which you are especially grateful, and give thanks.
2. *Review:* Recall the events of the day, from start to finish, noticing where you felt God's presence, and where you accepted or turned away from any invitations to grow in love.
3. *Sorrow:* Recall any actions for which you are sorry.
4. *Forgiveness:* Ask for God's forgiveness. Decide whether you want to reconcile with anyone you have hurt.

---

11   Baillie, J. (1961) *Christian Devotion: Addresses by John Baillie.* London: Oxford University Press. 77.

5. *Grace:* Ask God for the grace you need for the next day and an ability to see God's presence more clearly.[12]

There are versions and variations on this. Other examples include prayer for the illumination of the Holy Spirit to discern what those recollections might mean for the coming day. The desire for illumination is particularly apposite as the darkness falls.

The Anglican priest and physician Martin Israel advises dispassionate reflection on the course of the day's work, 'as we enter more deeply into our own being'.[13] Sometimes the assumption is that recollection at the end of the day is inevitably filled with dark thoughts and regrets. Israel keeps open the important reminder that this is not inevitable. Either way, 'the practice of meditating on major events in a day's life before one goes to bed is strongly to be recommended. How one has behaved is an excellent indication of one's state of spiritual health'. Matthew Linn describes his own preparation for sleep through the *Examen*. This involves reflecting on that which is most, and least, grateful for in the preceding day, seeking honestly to acknowledge pain and to receive love, 'then' he senses, 'I can usually fall asleep with a grateful heart'.[14] This, he believes, also affects his waking the next day with answers to problems from the previous night seeming much clearer in the morning. Ivens also commends his own practice as an aid to prayer, for spiritual directors and exercitants, 'after going to bed *as I am about to go to sleep* I will think for the space of a Hail Mary of the time I have to get up, and *for what purpose*, going over the exercise I have to make'.[15] Intentionality about waking and the coming day is as important as reviewing the day that is past.

The act of recollection of the past day is important. Sometimes that recollection highlights things for which we are not reconciled. Just as there is a deep desire for us to be reconciled to God and neighbour before we die so there is before we fall asleep too. Earlier eras had a far more acute sense that an individuals might die in sleep

---

12 Martin, J. (2012) *The Jesuit Guide to (Almost) Everything: A Spirituality for Real Life.* New York: HarperCollins. 97.

13 Israel, M. (1990) *Night Thoughts.* London: SPCK. 106.

14 Linn, D., Fabricant Linn, S., and Linn, M. (1995) *Sleeping With Bread: Holding What Gives You Life.* Mahwah, N.J: Paulist Press. 10.

15 Ivens, M. (1998) *Understanding the Spiritual Exercises.* Leominster: Gracewing. 65–6. Original italics.

– the fear of sudden death is not as widely shared, at least in the West today – so the imperative for reconciliation with God and neighbour may have been more pressing.

Recollection is not sufficient in itself without the move to reconciliation. Reconciliation before sleep has a long and important pedigree in Christian spirituality. It is an ancient feature of Compline, and may well have involved communal confession in the monastic context, hinted at in St Benedict's Rule. Benedict draws on Ephesians to say, 'If you have a dispute with someone, make peace with him before the sun goes down'. Dietrich Bonhoeffer expands on this to emphasise just how significant it is:

> It is perilous for the Christian to lie down to sleep with an unreconciled heart. Therefore, it is well that there be a special place for the prayer of brotherly forgiveness in every evening's devotion, that reconciliation be made and fellowship established anew.[16]

That is the corporate dimension of the necessity of reconciliation before sleep, but there is a personal and interior reason too. The sense that inner misery becomes magnified at night is shown by accounts of sleep such as those given by Roger Ekirch.[17] Reconciliation at bedtime is seen to be important because misery, distraction and anxiety can drive away sleep and good sleep means that misery is less likely to be magnified.

Martin Israel sees reconciliation before sleep as enabling 'a load, quite literally, to be lifted from our heart, where malign emotions tend to fester'. It is in this state that the *Nunc Dimittis* can be said and, 'we can retire to bed in peace'. Nonetheless Israel sees hopes and plans as, 'extinguished in the comforting oblivion of innocent sleep'. 'Sleep' he says, 'always brings us back to our childhood innocence, even when our daytime activities have been far from exemplary'. Such a statement is open to challenge and accusations of romanticism. As will be explored below, the person we are in sleep may be far from the (good) person we are awake. This gets to the heart of the relationship between waking and sleeping. Sleep takes us deep into our interior lives to become more the person God made us to be.

---

16   Bonhoeffer, *Life Together*, 56.
17   Ekirch, A.R. (2005) *At Day's Close: A History of Nighttime*. London: Weidenfeld and Nicolson.

Sleep hints at new creation precisely because of its capacity to give us the time and space to allow our transgressions and the wilfulness of our overbearing egos time to subside; the challenge is to connect the sleeping and waking life as one.

Your watch around us while we sleep

Compline begins with recollection, confession and reconciliation. The traditional hymn at Compline, Ante lucis terminum, opens up more themes about how sleep is hallowed and draws from the conviction that 'the Lord who watches over Israel will neither slumber nor sleep' (Psalm 121.4).

> Before the ending of the day,
> Creator of the world, we pray
> That you, with steadfast love, would keep
> Your watch around us while we sleep.

The conviction that God's watch continues even whilst the sleeper sleeps is a further expression of trust in grace. Nevertheless, there remains open the possibility that the long hours of the night also open the believer up to the possibility of less than godly interventions. When control is relinquished at the moment of sleep, the question is relinquishing control *to whom*? The theosomniac intention is that control is passed to God; but the hymn expresses the perennial fear, which is not restricted to pre-modern times, that somehow the onset of sleep opens up a dangerous or sinister world of influence upon the sleeper. The desire for protection is reinforced not in outward predatory threats but very much more the inner battle.

> From evil dreams defend our sight,
> From fears and terrors of the night;
> Tread underfoot our deadly foe
> That we no sinful thought may know.

The suspension of the senses allows for the possibility of 'evil dreams', 'fears and terrors' and 'sinful thoughts'. There is a long standing sense that 'evil dreams', for which may be read sexual dreams, will pervade and captivate the sleeper and that there will be responses, even involuntary ones, to the illusory images of the dream. This preoccupation draws more from the Augustinian anxiety about the suspension of reason and of the senses than it does from a purely scriptural origin. Bonhoeffer speaks eloquently of the inner threats, writing:

> We are struck by the frequency with which we encounter the prayer for preservation during the night from the devil, from terror and from an evil, sudden death. The ancients had a persistent sense of a man's helplessness while sleeping, of the kinship of sleep with death, of the devil's cunning in making man fall when he is defenceless.[18]

The sleeping hours hold both interior and external threats.

Sleep and Vulnerability

Thus far we have considered the inner threat that sleep poses. There is another primordial fear of death during sleep which is external, for instance killing by a partner or intruder. Indeed there are accounts of nocturnal murders in which the perpetrator has no recollection of committing the act. Qualitative evidence shows that those who suffer domestic violence very often report the deep sense of threat when they are asleep. Either the victim does not want to sleep before an abusive partner returns home possibly under the influence of alcohol or drugs, or cannot sleep until the other partner is asleep. Alongside that there is the sense of a threat that comes from the unknown.

Sleep is a profoundly vulnerable time for all creatures, and different creatures adopt varying strategies for safety according to species. Human sleep safety is dependent upon vigilance and trust. The vulnerability of sleep is due to it being a time when enemies can take you by surprise by surprise. Sleep is an act of faith and vulnerable time for which faith is needed.

The story of Samson and Delilah illustrates the vulnerability of sleep. It is set in the power struggle between Israel and the Philistines and played out between Samson and Delilah. The ways in which she attempts three times to coax Samson give away the secret of his strength have overtones of sexual power and a misogynistic portrayal of women. More pertinent here is that once Delilah has extracted Samson's secret it is whilst he is asleep that she is able to act on it.

---

18   Bonhoeffer, *Life Together*, 56.

The intimacy, abandonment and helplessness of sleep are deployed by Delilah as she lets '[Samson] fall asleep on her lap' (Judges 16.19a). When Delilah cries that the Philistines are upon him he awakes from sleep but is powerless. Power is exercised upon him *during sleep*. The downfall of Samson is not the only instance in the book of Judges in which a woman uses an opportunity brought about by sleep to defeat a man. Jael the wife of Heber takes a tent peg and hammers it into Sisera's temple taking her opportunity whilst 'he was lying fast asleep from weariness' (Judges 4.21). Sleep represents a time of opportunity for weaker persons and enemies to vanquish the strong and powerful. We have already seen Browne's reference to Jael and Sisera. He also draws on classical tradition as he refers to Themistocles who 'slew a soldier in his sleep' and is thus seen by Browne as a merciful executioner. The exercise of mercy by humans is a facet of power. Sleep has a demonstrable relationship with the exercise of power.

David and Abishai are awake at night when David spares Saul's life a second time during their internecine struggle. The helplessness of Saul is defined by the fact that whilst he has his weapons around him, 'Saul lay sleeping within the encampment' (1 Samuel 26.7). Just like the first time, when David cut off a piece of Saul's cloak to indicate that he had spared his life, David takes a trophy to indicate the same thing. He takes Saul's spear that is stuck in the ground next to his sleeping head. However not only is Saul asleep; his whole camp is asleep, '[n]o one saw it or knew it, nor did anyone awake; for they were all asleep, because a deep sleep from the LORD had fallen upon them' (1 Samuel 26.12b). This corporate sleep signifies Saul's increasing unfitness to be king: sleep is seemingly contagious. This is decisive because sleep is something that God has caused to fall upon them all. In Hebrew this is a 'deep sleep' (*tardema*) from God which causes Saul's sleep; the conclusion is that the Lord's favour clearly rests on David who also preserves his integrity by sparing the Lord's anointed. David is portrayed as alert and wake, in contrast to the sleeping Saul.

Sleep can be presented as, 'a potential haven in times of great adversity'. Stephen Jacobs notes the story from the sixth century, paralleled in the Quran (Surah 18 – Al Kahf: 9–26), of seven Christian youths, the 'Sleepers of Ephesus' who took refuge in a cave fleeing persecution from the Romans. They fell asleep, but did not wake for over three hundred years.[19] In this way sleep is a haven for the vulnerable rather than a posture of vulnerability.

From all dreams defend our sight

It would be an omission at this point not to refer in some detail to dreams. This book is about theology and sleep and not dreams per se, yet they are intimately connected. After all, *Ante lucis terminum* asks that the sleeper's eyes be protected from 'all ill dreams'. The interpretation of dreams exists within scripture, most notably in the case of Joseph (Genesis 37.5–11; 40–41.36) – although, as Joseph tells Pharaoh's officers in prison, the interpretation of dreams belongs to God (Genesis 40.8). There is also considerable popular literature on the interpretation of dreams, generated in part by a fusion of Biblicism and Jungian psychological interpretation, as well as serious academic work on dreams in scripture, notably by Diana Lipton.[20] Baillie speaks of a 'theology of dreams' as he explores the wider subject of sleep.

This is the point of connection between theosomnia and dreams. The theosomniac has to be open to the possibility of dreams and that dreams have the capacity to be uncomfortable, beautiful and/or decisive. This is not to make unsustainable claims about dreams or to accept wholesale Freudian or Jungian propositions about them. It is to say that such psychological insights may be useful, but also that sleep and dreams are related, and more than simply because sleep is the arena in which dreams take place.

The pastoral dimensions of dreams and dreaming will be referred to below. Suffice it to say at this stage that in scripture sleep and dreams are associated with theophany, a showing forth of God, most obviously through dreams, but not exclusively.

Prophetic visions are in some cases associated with sleep, but are not dreams in themselves; there is a qualitative difference between

---

19   Jacobs, S. (2012) 'Ambivalent Attitudes Towards Sleep in World Religions.' *Sleep: Multi-Professional Perspectives*, eds. Green, A and Westcombe, A. London: Jessica Kingsley Publishers, 250.

20   Lipton, D. (2009) *Revisions of the Night: Politics and Promises in the Patriarchal Dreams of Genesis.* London: Continuum.

them. When allied with sleep, dreams and visions give a sense of renewed purpose and direction. Such dreams convey the sense of God's mediation even during sleep. Lipton identifies ten clear-cut cases of dreaming in the book of Genesis alone. She notes that two episodes in particular have dream-like characteristics but are in fact called visions. These dreams of the patriarchs are also sources of hope for later generations because, '[i]t is only the involvement of the divine will that transforms chance parallels into messages of hope and reassurance concerning God's continuing love for Israel'. Lipton also refers to 'incubation dreams' which are placing oneself in the place and posture for the seeking out of dreams and visions. This means sleeping somewhere like a temple or shrine to gain proximity to nocturnal revelation from the deity. This is what Psalm 134 appears to allude to:

> Come bless the Lord, all you servants of the Lord,
> who stand by night *in the house of the Lord!*
> Lift up your hands *in the holy place*, and bless the Lord.
> May the Lord, maker of heaven and earth,
> bless you *from Zion.* (Psalm 134)

It may be that Samuel's sleeping and waking is in the context of an incubation dream because he was 'lying down in the temple' to sleep (1 Samuel 3). Either way, Samuel is not alone in receiving divine revelation whilst asleep. More often than not in scripture the sleeper dreams outside the temple setting. This is evident in the sleeping, dreaming and acting of Abraham and Jacob and Joseph, the guardian of Jesus.

Abraham, at this point known as Abram, has the first sleeping theophany (Genesis 15.12–16). Immediately prior to his sleep God made a covenant with him in a vision. In that vision he asks Abram to ponder the number of the stars, for such will his descendants be. As the sun was going down, even before the appearance of the stars, 'a deep sleep fell upon Abram, and a deep and terrifying darkness descended upon him' (Genesis 15.12). During his sleep it is revealed that his descendants will be numerous but they will also be exiles and oppressed and he himself will die 'in a good old age'.

One of Abraham's many descendants is Jacob who was a renowned sleeper and the first recorded Biblical dreamer. He is the father of Joseph: the name 'Joseph' is associated with dreams both in the Old and New Testament. At the end of a journey as the day closes Jacob's need is first to sleep:

> He came to a certain place and stayed there for the night, because the sun had set. Taking one of the stones of the place, he put it under his head and lay down in that place. (Genesis 28.11)

It is when he wakes up that Jacob makes a declaration of his awareness of the presence of God in his sleep and goes on with his journey with new purpose:

Then Jacob woke from his sleep and said, 'Surely the LORD is in this place—and I did not know it!' And he was afraid, and said, 'How awesome is this place! This is none other than the house of God, and this is the gate of heaven.' So Jacob rose early in the morning, and he took the stone that he had put under his head and set it up for a pillar and poured oil on the top of it (Genesis 28. 16–18).

In this way Jacob's waking life corresponds to his sleeping life. His son Joseph is, famously, a dreamer, but less is said of his sleep. There is a greater connection on sleep between Jacob and the later Joseph, the guardian of Jesus. Jacob's 'night vision', a dream as Lipton sees it, tells the same message to Jacob, as to Joseph of Nazareth, that he is to go down to Eygpt where he will raise up a great nation. Joseph in the Hebrew Bible is perhaps the most flamboyant dreamer and interpreter of dreams. Nevertheless it is the New Testament Joseph who much more resembles Jacob because it is a feature of his to sleep, to wake and then to act on the communication that God makes through his angel (cf Matthew 1.24).

Baillie suggests that dreams are generally not understood any more as 'premonitory of the unborn future' but more likely to be 'uprisings from the half-buried past'. Sleep is the arena for such uprisings. Gregory of Nyssa connects the activity of the waking life with the irruptions of dreams referring to the dreams of the butler and baker in the Joseph cycle as being the space in which, 'each supposing himself in sleep to be engaged in those services with which he was busied when he was awake: for the images of their customary occupations imprinted on the prescient element of their soul'. Dreams appear to connect waking and sleeping in ways that are little understood yet feel immediate.

The Christian contention is that God can be with the disciple even in sleep and also in dreams. In *The Pilgrim's Progress*, Mercy's mother, Christiana explains:

> We need not, when a-bed, lie awake to talk with God; He can visit us while we sleep, and cause us then to hear His voice. Our heart oft-times wakes when we sleep, and God can speak to that, either by words, by proverbs, by signs and similitudes, as well as if one was awake.[21]

Not all dreams are threatening ones, although as Ancoli-Israel notes, 'Dreams are not always benign' and, '[n]ightmares hound some of the figures in the Bible'.

Defence from 'all ill dreams and fantasies' is the plea and declaration of intent in *Ante lucis terminum*. If sleep represents a loss of control, then we might ask, 'a loss of control *from* whom and *to* whom?' The anxiety of demonic influence during sleep revealed in dreams is a longstanding one. Karl Rahner, speaking to an interlocutor, refers to the lurking, 'terror of losing consciousness before the *adversaries vester diabolus, quarens quem devoret*... You are of course familiar with the prayer which we say from the breviary before going to sleep'.[22] He is referring to 1 Peter 5.8,9, the default scripture verse used at Compline.

Prayer practices before sleep are, as it were, an inoculation against demonic influence whilst the ego is subdued. Baillie echoes this ancient strand of thought saying, 'it is certain that if there were no evil in our waking souls, there would be no evil in our dreams'. The way in which control can be exercised over dreams is, 'the proper direction of our thoughts before we retire'.

Compline, the *Examen*, evening hymns and prayers before bed are an attempt at the proper directing not only of thoughts, but of the

---

21   Baillie, Christian Devotion, quoting from John Bunyan, *The Pilgrim's Progress*, 75.

22   Rahner, K. (1967) *Theological Investigations (III): Theology of the Spiritual Life*, trans. Kruger, K-H and B. London: Darton, Longman and Todd, 224. 'Sobrii estote et vigilate, quia adversaries vester diabolus tamquam leo rugiens circuit, quarens quem devoret', 'Be sober, be vigilant, for your adversary the devil is prowling round like a roaring lion, looking for someone to devour'. (1 Pet. 5.8).

body and the spirit before sleep. *Ante lucis terminum* prays for God's watchfulness and protection, so that with the 'barriers down' the sleeper who, in faith, relinquishes control is possessed by the Trinity and not the enemy. This is an act of trust.

The Psalms of Compline

The Psalms of Compline – traditionally Psalms 4, 91 and 134 – express the themes outlined above. The first two are very much more exterior in their approach to sleep than the third. So, for instance, in psalm 4, 'in peace I will lie down and sleep, for it is you Lord, only, who make me dwell in safety'. Psalm 91 goes further in referring to the way in which God will 'cover you with his wings and you shall be safe under his feathers; his faithfulness shall be your buckler and shield'. That certainly evokes a sense of first innocency of the child tucked safely within the warmth and protection of the parent; a reassuring image of sleep. The threat later in the psalm deploys a martial image of the arrow that flies by day and 'you shall not be afraid of any terror by night' or 'of the pestilence that stalks in darkness'. The denouement of the psalm begins with the reference to God giving, 'his angels charge over you'. Angelic protection is a recurring theme in piety and hymnody, for example, Reginald Heber's evening hymn 'God who madest earth and heaven' draws on this image, 'May thine angel-guards defend us.' Likewise a prayer attributed to St Augustine: 'Keep watch dear Lord with those who wake or watch or weep this night, and give your angels charge over those who sleep'. It is a verse from Psalm 4 draws together the strands of Compline very effectively, 'In peace I will lie down and sleep, for it is you Lord, only, who make me dwell in safety' (Psalm 4.8)

The Compline not only assumes and invites God's watchful and graceful protection but also offers a response to it. This response is a conscious offering by the sleeper of the sleeper's self to the God who already watches over the sleep. Hence in the responsory of Compline the phrase, 'Into your hands, O Lord, I commend my spirit' is repeated.

Guard us while sleeping

The relationship between sleep and eschatology will be explored further, but in this examination of Compline we see in the gospel canticle, the Nunc Dimittis (Luke 2.29–32), has an eschatological dimension. Simeon entrusts himself into God's hands having seen the salvation revealed in Jesus Christ. The use of this canticle at Compline suggests a connection between death and salvation and the daily lying down to sleep. Furthermore Simeon can also usefully be seen as the antitype of Eli, who slept in the Temple and failed to detect God's presence when Samuel could. Simeon the elderly temple dweller is awake and alert, as is Anna, to the coming presence of God.

The antiphon to the canticle alludes to death, both as a metaphor for the act of sleeping, but holds very clearly the sense that one may never wake from sleep.

> Save us, O Lord, while waking,
> and guard us while sleeping,
> that awake we may watch with Christ
> and asleep may rest in peace.[23]

Reginald Heber renders this more explicitly:

> Guard us, waking, guard us sleeping;
> And, when we die,
> May we in thy mighty keeping
> All peaceful lie:
> When the last dread call shall wake us,
> Do not thou our God forsake us...

And Bishop Thomas Ken (1637–1711) in his hymn says 'Teach me to live, that I may dread the grave as little as my bed'.

The canticle itself is suitable for the night as it speaks of time to go in peace and illumination that comes from God: it is very *theosomniac* in tone because it hallows the sleep of eternity as much as the sleep of the coming night.

---

23 Archbishops' Council, The. *Common Worship Daily Prayer*. London: Church House Publishing, 2007. 342.

Sleep and death

As Ken's words suggest, sleep and mortality have long been interconnected. Portrayals of a deathbed scene in art classically illustrate this: with images of weeping relatives around the bed of the dying person. They juxtapose the place of sleep with the sleep of death. Browne's insight into sleep as, 'a moderating point between life and death' finds echoes in philosophical thinking about sleep. Theology goes further, as seen in Browne as he connects sleep, death and resurrection. 'We term sleep a death' he says, and continues:

> and yet it is our waking that kills us and destroys those spirits which are the house of life. 'Tis indeed a part of life that best expresseth death, for every man truly lives so long as he acts his nature, or some way makes good faculties of himself.[24]

In his survey of Jacques Derrida's treatment of sleep, Morgan Wortham calls it, 'the suspensive medium of life-death'. Any consideration of sleep inevitably touches questions around the anticipation of or glimpses into death. A great human terror is that of being asleep and mistaken for dead; the opposite of the experience of Lazarus and Jairus' daughter. The haunting fear of the mortal being is the end of life and total annihilation. For those who live in the hope of resurrection this is also hard but is a reality faced daily in prayer, hymnody and reflection. In his poem 'Death' George Herbert writes,

> Therefore we can go die as sleep, and trust
> Half that we have
> Unto an honest faithful grave;
> Making our pillows either down, or dust. [25]

The image of the pillow as dust or down draws sleep and death together as sides of the same coin, but more than that, as John Drury notes, 'we can look forward to a happy doomsday resurrection when death's grizzly bones will be clothed with beautiful flesh'.[26]

---

24 Browne, *Religio Medici*. 92.
25 Herbert, G. (1995) *The Complete English Works*. Ed Pasternak Slater, A. London: David Campbell Publishers. 182.
26 Drury, J. (2013) *Music at Midnight: The Life and Poetry of George Herbert*. London: Penguin Books. 254.

Tombs often give insights in views of death. Examples of seventeenth and eighteenth century tombs bear this out and portrays the deceased as sleeping. In Wheathampstead Church, Herfordshire the lord and lady recline on pillows as if dozing off to sleep and discussing who will turn the light out. In St John the Baptist, High Barnet, the tomb of Thomas Ravenscroft depicts him in a tomb that resembles a four poster bed, and there are countless others.

Each night is a powerful reminder of the ephemeral nature of the past day's achievements or ambition. The night focuses anxieties of annihilation and the sense that the value of a human life may never be appreciated or come to anything. Peterson and Seligman give a framework for the assessment of fulfilment in life through their 'deathbed test':

> How might people, if able to collect their thoughts, complete the sentence: 'I wish I had been able to spend more time…' It is doubtful that anyone would say 'visiting Disneyland' or 'eating butter pecan ice-cream'. These activities are fun but not fulfilling. At least in our society, the deathbed test is instead met by activities that pertain to work and love broadly construed, as in 'I wish I had spent more time getting to know my children and being kind to my friends.' In a less secular society, people might wish to that they had spent more time praising God and giving thanks.[27]

That 'test' draws from a keen awareness of mortality and the limited nature of life but also the nature of fulfilment. Sleep both draws attention to mortality, but also offers the possibility that the darkness and lack of awareness need not mean annihilation and nothingness. Rather, sleep becomes a time for a celebration of mortality and resting in the fulfilment given in the day.

St John Climacus, writing in the sixth century, hints at an understanding of some of the pastoral issues around sleep and the mortality of the body:

> Sleep is a natural state. It is also an image of death and a respite of the senses. Sleep is one, but like desire it has many sources. That is to say, it comes from nature, from food, from demons, or perhaps

---

27   Peterson, C. and Seligman, M.E.P. (2004) *Character Strengths and Virtues: A Handbook and Classification*, Oxford: Oxford University Press, 2004. 17.

in some degree even from prolonged fasting by which the weakened flesh is moved to long for repose.[28]

Climacus is aware of the frailty and lack of permanence of the body in which sleep dwells. Writing on the necessity of a daily discipline of life and prayer, William Perkins (1558–1602) wrote:

> And when thou liest down, let that be the last also, for thou knowest not whether fallen asleep, thou shalt ever rise again alive. Good therefore it is that thou shouldest give up thyself into the hands of God, whilst thou art waking.[29]

Perkins is acutely aware of his mortality. His awareness of his mortality when awake informs understanding of sleep.

Lying down awaiting the onset of sleep is a time when many people have recalled their mortality, as Herbert, quoted above said that, 'in sleep we see foul death, and live'. Prayers before bed often contain ambiguity about sleep and death, such as that from Compline, 'The Lord almighty grant us a quiet night and a perfect end'. The 'end' may be the end of the day, or it may also be the 'end' of mortal life. Drawing on the death of Jesus, and therefore meditating on human mortality and death, the collect for Compline on a Friday is addressed to the second person of the Trinity:

> who at this evening hour lay in the tomb
> and so hallowed the grave
> to be a bed of hope for all who put their trust in you:
> give us such sorrow for our sins,
> which were the cause of your passion,
> that when our bodies lie in the dust,
> our souls may live with you for ever.[30]

The recurrent inseparability of sleep and mortality articulated in prayer appears in the eighteenth century *New England Primer*.

---

28 Luibhied, C. and Russell, N. (1982) *John Climacus: The Ladder of Divine Ascent.* London: SPCK Publishing. 194.

29 Rowell, G., Stevenson, K. and Williams, R., eds. (2001) *Love's Redeeming Work: The Anglican Quest for Holiness.* Oxford: Oxford University Press. 122.

30 Common Worship, *Daily Prayer.* 347.

Now I lay me down to sleep,
I pray thee, Lord, my soul to keep;
If I should die before I wake,
I pray thee, Lord, my soul to take.[31]

Fear of the night and darkness, and the response in sleep is tackled head on by prayer and worship practices that call on God's watchfulness and light. Sleep alerts human beings to the finiteness of existence and therefore to their mortality.

There is hope however as we prepare to sleep. Kallistos Ware sees sleep as a 'little death' that anticipates the 'greater death'. Three aspects of this greater death are always to be kept in view: death is closer to us than we imagine; it is deeply unnatural, contrary to the divine plan, yet deeply natural; and, it is a separation that is no separation. Ware connects proximity of death with sleep because it fits into a death-life pattern; something that is visible in other stages of human development and in the natural world. In this way the fear of death is diminished if it is to be likened to falling asleep, 'we are not afraid to drop off each night, because we expect to wake up once more next morning'.

For tranquil sleep

To the question how do I best prepare for sleep, the theosomniac's answer is, in prayer. This may be in the formal Liturgy of the Hours or more informally. The theosomniac's goal is one that may seem unattainable, but for St John Cassian (c360–435) the constantly repeated prayer, 'Come to my help, O God; Lord, hurry to my rescue' (Psalm 40.13) wards off the temptations of the world, the flesh and the devil, such that, 'sleep should come upon you as you meditate on this verse until as a result of your habit of resorting to its words you get in the habit of repeating them even in your slumbers'. To say that prayer is the best preparation for sleep is not to prescribe a magical inoculation against insomnia or bad dreams, rather it is about the disposition and posture of the mind and spirit in preparation for the fall of sleep. This is why instinctively, it would seem, many people

---

31 Wikipedia *The New England Primer*. Accessed on 25/9/14 at http://en.wikipedia.org/wiki/The_New_England_Primer

have sought to pray before bed, not least in shaping the practices of children in prayer. There are treasuries of books with children's bedtime prayers.

The deeper point of prayer before sleep, like Cassian's, is captured by Bonhoeffer as he concludes his reflections on praying before sleep:

> Most remarkable is and profound is the ancient church's prayer that when our eyes are closed in sleep God may nevertheless keep our hearts awake. It is the prayer that God may dwell with us and in us even though we are unconscious of his presence, that he may keep our hearts pure and holy in spite of all the cares and temptations of the night, to make our hearts ever alert to his call and, like the boy Samuel, answer him even in the night…Even in sleep God can perform his wonders upon us or evil bring us to destruction. So we pray at evening:
>
> > When our eyes with sleep are girt,
> > Be our hearts to thee alert;
> > Shield us, Lord, with thy right arm,
> > Save us from sin's dreadful harm. (Luther)[32]

Israel further picks up on the instinctive desire to pray before sleep:

> the secret of falling asleep, like so many activities, is to let go, quite consciously falling into the sustaining arms of God. Sleep comes as a peak of untroubled faith; it is the point where God is proved in the work of acceptance.[33]

He articulates this in a prayer:

> I thank you Lord, for your beautiful gift of sleep. I pray that my life may be so dedicated to your glory and the service of my brothers that I may bring them that love that finds its proof in tranquil sleep.

---

32 Bonhoeffer, *Life Together*. 54.
33 Israel, *Night Thoughts*. 111.

2

I WILL LIE DOWN AND SLEEP

We have considered the ways in which sleep is approached in Christian practices and how they aid the creation of a spiritual posture which mirrors the needful physical posture we adopt in order to sleep and to entrust. So what of the time of sleep itself? It is inevitably hard to account for the experience of sleep whilst we are sleeping, both from an experiential and theological point of view. As we saw earlier, EEG and scientific insights tell us about brain patterns while we sleep, but cannot tell us what it is like to sleep. Jeff Warren's book *Head Trip* shows that there are ways to capture sleep experiences that are almost concurrent with sleep, but one has to wake to describe them.[1] All this means that to account for sleep we enter into a speculative mode and we do so from the waking state.

In the Introduction the notion of *theosomnia* was describable in the context of the practices around sleep, those things that we can be aware of and alert to whether preparing for sleep or waking from it. When it comes to being asleep we have to acknowledge a certain letting go. The account *theosomnia* gives of sleep has to be framed in a different way, gazing upon the sleeping body as it were. The theological priority is to consider the figure of the sleeping Christ. The sleep of Jesus Christ is the source from which we begin to consider the way in which the *theosomniac* sleeps.

This chapter uses the sleep of Jonah and Jesus as ways to consider the nature of sleep from a Christian point of view. As we start to consider the sleep of Jesus, we must first also consider the sleep of Jonah, because the Synoptic Gospels portray the sleeping Jesus in the midst of the storm on the Sea of Galilee (see Matthew 8.23–27, Mark 4.35–41 and Luke 8.22–25). This is typological as we find in the story of Jonah one who also sleeps in a storm on a boat. The parallels juxtapose the two sleepers: one, Jesus, who embodies a sleep that embodies the deep peace he has received through fidelity to

---

1   Warren, J. (2007) *Head Trip: A Fantastic Romp Through 24 Hours in the Life of Your Brain.* Oxford: Oneworld.

his purpose; and the other, Jonah, who is in flight and sleeps in a sleep of abandon to avoid the consequences of the purpose to which he has been called. The respective sleep of Jonah and Jesus reveals some of the tensions in a Christian account of sleep.

We will then explore the way in which Thérèse of Lisieux (1873–1897) contemplates the image of the sleeping Christ. The contemplative and mystical theme continues in the work of Gregory the Great (540–604) and Bernard of Clairvaux (1090–1153) as two representative contemplatives who reflect on a key text in a Christian understanding of sleep from the Song of Songs, 'I sleep, yet my heart wakes', which synthesises the physical act of being asleep with the spiritual process that may be going on inside. It gives sleep a sacramental character, as an outward and visible sign of an inward and spiritual grace: the sleeping body of Jesus is the exemplar of this and so is profoundly important to the *theosomniac*.

Jesus Christ the sleeper

Some texts from the Hebrew Scriptures frame the theological qualities of sleep. They embody resistance to anxiety and fearfulness and embracing trustfulness and confidence:

> And I will grant peace in the land, and you shall lie down [to sleep], and no one shall make you afraid. (Leviticus 26.6)

> If you sit down, you will not be afraid;
> when you lie down your sleep will be sweet.
> Do not be afraid of sudden panic,
> or of the storm that strikes the wicked. (Proverbs 3.24–26)

> And you will have confidence, because there is hope; you will be protected and take your rest in safety. You will lie down, and no one will make you afraid; many will entreat your favour. (Job 11.18, 19)

This does not represent the idealisation of sleep; rather it acknowledges that not all sleeping is characterised by trust and peace. These verses exemplify the virtuous sleep. It is not a sleep prompted by sloth and is certainly a sleep that is not characterised by fear. These texts can be claimed as qualitatively descriptive of the sleep of Jesus and of the trusting, *theosomniac*, disciple. Nevertheless not all sleep is without anxiety, and often is elusive precisely because of fear and anxiety.

The sleep of Jonah

As the story of Jonah's sleep is considered, we will see why it is a helpful foil to understanding the sleep of Jesus on the boat. First is the situation that got Jonah to be on the boat in the first place and why he slept as the storm blew up. Jonah was fleeing from what the Lord had commanded him to do. This has raised the question amongst interpreters as to what Jonah's sleep signifies. The judgement is split. Jonah's sleep has been viewed as a sign of his disobedience; a curse because of his flight from God; as a symptom of deep fear or vulnerability; and conversely as a sign of serenity.

Jonah's sleep has prompted other reflections about how God watches over the sleeper. This has often been in contrast to Jesus' sleep. For example, Phillip Cary suggests that God would not allow 'the Israelite unconscious in the inner part of the ship' to succumb to the violence of the sea, and then he notes 'a yet more representative Israelite who also slept in a boat threatened by a great storm that terrified everyone else on board'.[2] Cary contrasts the sleeping Jesus with Jonah: 'the obedient prophet identifying with the disobedient'. Sleep in this instance can be characterised as a comfort to the obedient and a tranquilliser to the disobedient.

Both Jonah and Jesus are awakened from their sleep; Jonah having been searched out sleeping below deck, and Jesus on the deck with the disciples. The connection between Jonah and Jesus in the storm is not a new one. Cyril of Jerusalem (313–386) weaves the two together and draws out further sleep as a euphemism for death and waking and as a euphemism for resurrection:

> And when we examine the story of Jonah, great is the force of the resemblance. Jesus was sent to preach repentance; Jonah also was sent: but whereas the one fled, not knowing what should come to pass; the other came willingly, to give repentance unto salvation. Jonah was asleep in the ship, and snoring amidst the stormy sea; while Jesus also slept, the sea, according to God's providence, began

---

2   Cary, P. (2008) *Jonah*. London: SCM Press, p.50.

to rise, to show in the sequel the might of Him who slept. To the one they said, 'Why are you sleeping? Arise, call your God, that God may save us'; but in the other case they say unto the Master, 'Lord, save us.' Then they said, 'Call upon thy God'; here they say, 'save Thou'. But the one says, 'Take me, and cast me into the sea; so shall the sea be calm unto you'; the other, Himself rebuked the winds and the sea, and there was a great calm. The one was cast into a whale's belly: but the other of His own accord went down, where the invisible whale of death is. And He went down of His own accord, that death might cast up those whom he had devoured, according to that which is written, 'I will ransom them from the power of the grave; and from the hand of death I will redeem them'.[3]

Cyril's reflections take us beyond our immediate concern (Chapter 3 will examine the eschatological character of sleep) but it reveals a bind for theology in considering sleep. Is sleep essentially a negative thing, as Cyril suggests when he describes Jonah's snoring, or is it essentially a good thing, which Jesus' appears to be? Or can it be within a Christian account of sleep? These are recurring questions and illustrate the value judgements placed on sleep. This takes us to a contradiction at the heart of Christian views of sleep.

For a negative judgement of sleep we need look no further than the fictional Father Mapple, in Melville's *Moby-Dick*. He is acutely aware of the seriousness of Jonah's disobedience. Mapple sees Jonah as 'most contemptible and worthy of all scorn' as he seeks a ship bound for Tarshish. He then describes the chaotic scene on the boat. His speech echoes the description of 'they that go down in ships' in Psalm 107 who when 'the stormy wind ariseth [those on board] reel to and fro' (Psalm 107.25, 27). But, Mapple continues, as 'every plank thunders with trampling feet right over Jonah's head; in all this tumult, Jonah sleeps his hideous sleep'. The hideousness of the sleep is the predicament of Jonah and the sailors; it is the consequence of Jonah's disobedience.

Jerome (347–420) sees Jonah's sleep quite differently. He describes Jonah's sleep as 'the serenity of the soul of the prophet'.[4] He sleeps serenely because neither tempest nor dangers disturb him'.

---

3   St Cyril of Jerusalem, *Catechetical Lectures*, XIV, 17.
4   St Jerome, *In Ionam Prophetam*, col. 1125.

For Gregory of Nazianzus (328–390), sleep in the book of Jonah is a place of refuge and inner safety. Gregory is a little more nuanced in his account. He suggests that Jonah's sleep is one of self-protection:

> ...accordingly [Jonah] left the watchtower of joy, for this is the meaning of Joppa in Hebrew, I mean his former dignity and reputation, and flung himself into the deep of sorrow: and hence he is tempest-tossed, and falls asleep, and is wrecked, and aroused from sleep, and taken by lot, and confesses his flight, and is cast into sea, and swallowed, but not destroyed, by the whale.[5]

Given Jonah's prophetic status and typological significance, there is a desire for his sleep to be somehow Christological, something that Father Mapple is not so concerned about. For him the negative account of sleep constitutes both a moral exhortation and contrast to the sleep of Jesus.

A contemporary interpretation of Jonah's sleep draws on exegetical and psychological insight. James Alison comments that 'Jonah in full flight is at the centre of a storm, yet he is asleep in the bowels of the ship'. Alison's account of Jonah's sleep is that

> he doesn't appreciate at all that there is a storm going on, even less that it has something to do with him. Like so many who are in flight, he has managed to cut himself off from the pain and violence which is his, so the violence rages around a superficially imperturbable and serene centre.[6]

Alison's reading of Jonah is that he is a disturbed man, in flight from something deep inside himself. In this account, it is a sleep of depression. The retreat into sleep in Jonah's case is a way in which he copes with both pride and shame in his life. Alison's reading of Jonah's sleep is quite unlike Father Mapple's.

There is a catechetical and homiletic point to be drawn from Jonah's sleep. Cary seeks to do this by suggesting that contemporary believers resemble 'disobedient Jonah' without being aware of it. This is because, he suggests, we are 'quite capable of sleeping through disasters and unconscious of the ruin we bring upon our neighbors'.

---

5   *The Sacred Writings of Gregory Nazianzus*, Oration 2, 109.
6   Alison, J. (2001) *Faith Beyond Resentment: Fragments Catholic and Gay*. London: Darton, Longman and Todd, p.88.

The portrayal of sleep in the book of Jonah is generally overlooked by commentators. Sleep is being used as a metaphor and, as we will see similarly in Chapter 2, it can be used positively and negatively according to circumstances. In general, sleep is portrayed negatively in Jonah. Despite that, it also touches deeper theological streams. Thus Alison treats Jonah's sleep as a way of dealing with truthfulness. Sleep becomes a theologically therapeutic approach to reconciling human personality to itself. Cary also uses the narrative figuratively as he speaks of Jonah's descent. The descent is physically into the hold of the ship, but also figuratively descending into a place of apparent safety: a descent into sleep. Of course, Jonah has further to go: his descent is to continue right down to 'the roots of the mountains' (Jonah 2.6) having been cast into the deep. Jonah had descended 'to the furthest recesses of the ship, perhaps down into the cargo hold, [and] has laid himself down and then fallen into even deeper sleep'. Jonah truly *falls* into sleep. There is a further crossover into the Gospels, since the 'sign of Jonah' (Matthew 12.38–42; Luke 11.29–32), in which, as we have seen, sleep is integral. This is the one sign that Jesus declares that his generation may have.

Lord, save us, we are perishing

Typically, the 'majority report' is that the difference between Jonah sleeping on a boat and Jesus is that Jonah's sleep is induced by fear, fright, terror and flight, whilst Jesus' sleep is induced by peace and acceptance of the Father's will. The incident on the Sea of Galilee also speaks of the disciples' fearfulness of sleep in a situation of danger. That fear is perfectly legitimate when viewed from a pragmatic point of view. The way in which the disciples respond to Jesus being asleep raises questions: How would the sleep of Jesus materially diminish the ability of experienced fishermen to bring their boat under control? What was behind their plea to wake Jesus from sleep? Jesus' sleep is not viewed neutrally by the disciples, and we cannot consider Jesus' sleep in isolation from the disciples' reaction.

Jacobs interprets the disciples' insomnia on the boat as a sign of their deep-seated fear rather than the more prosaic interpretation that they were sailing the boat and they were in a storm: they needed to be awake. However, Jacobs' question echoes that of Karl Rahner:

'could it not be the case...that the longing to avoid death which remains to us from Adam as a sublime atavism expresses itself also as a resistance to sleep?'[7] Jesus' sleep is pointing beyond the pragmatic to deeper realities which the disciples could not see at that point.

On waking, the question Jesus asks the disciples is one of rebuke, but not about their decision not to sleep – it is about their continued fearfulness in his presence, albeit his sleeping presence. Jesus the sleeper embodies peace and vigilance even in his sleeping state, and the disciples should have known that, hence the rebuke. There is a marked contrast (to be explored further in Chapter 2) between Jesus asleep on the boat when the disciples wake him, and the disciples asleep in the Garden of Gethsemane when he wakes the disciples. Jacobs also notes this contrast:

> In that case [Gethsemane], a demonstration of faith demands perpetual vigilance (to be awake) to the sacred, whereas the account of the stormy sea suggests that faith in the sacred requires the adherent to relax their vigilance (sleep), no matter what the profane circumstances might be, and failure to sleep signifies faithlessness.[8]

Jacobs uses the language of the 'sacred' in a generalised way. For Christian theology, it is the person of Jesus Christ to whom the disciples principally relate, hence the rebuke in both situations.

Again we encounter the contradictory evaluations of sleep. On Galilee fear keeps the disciples awake; in Gethsemane fear compels them to sleep. This echoes the human experience of the maelstrom of 'fears and fantasies' that makes no action, willed or unwilled, entirely neutral. The anxiety of the disciples is various: physical fear of the storm; fear of what Jesus calls them to encounter and experience; and they fear also his ability to sleep and take rest in the midst of the storm. This is counter to the Old Testament texts above and leads us on to explore the nature of Jesus' sleep on the boat.

---

7   Rahner, K. (1967) *Theological Investigations III: Theology of the Spiritual Life.* London: Darton, Longman and Todd, p.222.
8   Jacobs, S. (2012) 'Ambivalent Attitudes Towards Sleep in World Religions.' In A. Green and A. Westcombe, A (eds) *Sleep: Multi-Professional Perspectives.* London: Jessica Kingsley Publishers, p.254.

But Jesus was asleep

The incident on the Sea of Galilee leads us to consider Jesus' own sleeping and his waking. Neither can be dissociated from his action on waking, that of calming the storm.

For our purposes, it is the consideration of the fact that Jesus sleeps, rather than the stilling of the storm, that is important. This takes us to the heart of the nature of Jesus Christ, true God, true human. As previously noted, the psalms testify that it is not in God's nature to sleep (Psalm 121.4), so when referring to the sleeping on the boat Ben Quash comments that 'sleeping is something that *creatures* do, but which – in traditional ways of thinking – God *doesn't* do'.[9] And, as also previously noted, the psalms also concede that, even if it is not in God's nature to sleep, there are times when it is perceived that God is or has been asleep, hence the plea in the psalms and on the disciples' lips to 'Rouse yourself! Why do you sleep, O Lord?' (Psalm 44.23).

The stilling of the storm is often seen as associating Jesus with the creative power of God. Thus, Jesus Christ, the Lord of all creation, is the one who sleeps and who, in the Sabbath which crowns the creation, gives sleep. Sabbath is a creative rest, not an abandonment into sleep. Nancy's interpretation is that God slept, but not because he was tired, or it was a contingent feature of who he is, but rather:

> At the very first, the one who uttered Fiat lux must somewhere have taken part in sleep. God must have slept, on the first night, for without that he could not next day have differentiated the rest of his work. He slept every night and he still sleeps upon all those nights that separate all the days he continues to make, or that continue to make themselves with him.[10]

Indeed, Nancy goes further by suggesting that 'sleep is divine' not as an object of worship, but that it is of God, 'for this reason, and the most uniquely divine thing revealed in it is the suspense of creative speech'.

---

9   Quash, B. (2012) *Abiding*. London: Bloomsbury Publishing, p.205.
10   Nancy, J-L. (2009) *The Fall of Sleep*, trans. C. Mandell. New York: Fordham University Press.

For Charles Péguy in *Basic Verities*, sleep is a thing of beauty (and behold it was good) such that he can say:

Sleep is the friend of man.
Sleep is the friend of God.
Sleep is perhaps the most beautiful thing I have created.
I myself rested on the seventh day.
He whose heart is pure, sleeps
And he who sleeps has a pure heart.

So it is not that God is 'tired' in the sense that a person becomes tired and so needs to sleep: rather, human rest and sleep is from the Creator, and sleep is virtuous because of its divine origin.

Morgan Wortham says of Nancy's perspective:

For Nancy the 'divinity' of sleep entails a profound openness to 'this ex nihilo that light first drove back to the heart of darkness in the movement by which it sprang from it' (p.24). Sleep, in other words, opens onto the nothing that existed before the bursting forth of light in creation worked to partition its undifferentiated expanse, re-describing it as mere darkness, figurelessness, absence of form or thing-hood.[11]

Thus the themes of darkness and light, and night and day, are bound up in the Hebrew account of creation. Sleep takes its place in this enduring pattern and rhythm of the night and day, so much so that it can be said that the 'doing' of sleep is the 'undoing' of the night and of the darkness: 'night as frontier', as Murray Melbin has put it. Sleep is the differentiator used by the Creator, but that does not restrict or compromise the Creator.

This use of sleep as differentiator is completely unlike an example recounted by V.S. Naipaul from Hinduism: 'every day Shiva watches over the world, but there is one day when he falls asleep, and Hindus on that day (or night) have to stay awake, to watch'.[12] Jesus Christ, the Incarnate Word, in his divinity has no requirement to sleep, but in his humanity does sleep. As Son of Man, Jesus does not resist sleep

11   Morgan Wortham, S. (2013) *The Poetics of Sleep: From Aristotle to Nancy*. London: Bloomsbury, p.137.
12   Naipaul, V.S. (1990) *India: A Million Mutinies Now*. London: William Heinemann, p.227.

but succumbs to it as we all do. However, Jesus' sleep recasts what it means to sleep and in so doing straddles the apparent contradictions in sleep as positive or negative. This is the deepest source for *theosomnia*.

So in the incident on the Sea of Galilee we see the *theosomniac* Christ sleeping in intentionally hallowed sleep that is dependent on the Father and not on the needs of another person. This sleep embodies the intimacy of the relationship of the Father and the Son, and thereby invites those who are God's children by adoption and grace to share in that trustful sleep. It acknowledges the incarnate character of who Jesus is as Son of God. Seen alongside Gethsemane, it also speaks of the need for vigilance in the waking and sleeping life. *Theosomnia* holds the positives and negatives of sleep together, since in Christ they are recast to be integral aspects to how we live as waking and sleeping disciples.

Jesus is roused from the serenity of sleep and then restores calm, evocative of the Sabbath rest. Jesus' sleep embodies *shalom*. And herein lies the rub. Jesus' sleep is read by the disciples as at best an indication of lack of care and at worst a lack of solidarity with them in their peril. Quash suggests that Jesus' sleep could also be seen as an expression of casualness but he sees it as 'an expression of *peace*'. This helpfully reinforces the intentionality of Jesus' sleep. This is a *purposeful sleep* of repose in adversity. Jesus' sleep is the sleep of innocence, the sleep of peace that a fallen and restless world finds elusive. Furthermore, Jesus' sleep is not treated as a diminishment of sovereignty, but rather serves as a foil to associate him with the creative power of God as he is able to wake to rebuke the elements and calm the storm.

Contemplating the sleeping Jesus: Thérèse of Lisieux

Thérèse of Lisieux contemplates the sleeping Christ and draws out the themes of vulnerability and abandonment in sleep. Thérèse moves contemplation of the sleeping Jesus into adoration and associates it with the genre of the lullaby. Lullabies draw the infant into sleep, and so it is in the image of mother and child that we begin.

Mother and child

In the primal and powerful image of the Madonna and Child a gaze of adoration is present. Often, images of the nativity in the classic western tradition show the Mother, Mary, gazing adoringly upon the Christchild, who may be portrayed awake or asleep. In eastern iconography, the attention of the gaze varies. In the *Virgin Eleousa* (Virgin of Loving Kindness), Christ gazes at Mary who in turn gazes out to the face of the beholder of the icon. In some of the *Eleousa* icons Mary returns her son's gaze. Sara Maitland describes the 'heartbreaking clarity' of the mutuality of mother and child in the night feed of 'a full and contented baby falling asleep at the empty and contented breast'.[13] She comments of the mother, in a counterpoint to waking, that 'you are awake to experience it solely and only because you are experiencing it'. Sleep is denied the mother because 'if the feeding were not happening you would almost certainly be asleep, be absent from consciousness in a very real way'. Maternal watchfulness over the sleeping contented child is very powerful.

Lullaby and the sleeping child

The lullaby is typically about inducing sleep in the infant. Albert Doja notes that, 'lullabies appease infants because they find in these melopoeias the carnal contact of the voice they perceived *in utero*, accompanied by the swaying of the crib, which was until recently that of the maternal body in motion'.[14] Nancy comments that these rocking movements are integral to the fall of sleep 'because sleep in its essence is a rocking, not a stable, motionless state'.[15] The relationship between the mother and sleeping child is established before the birth of the child and continues into infancy.

The mother watches vigilantly, gazing upon the face of her child whilst the child plays and sleeps. Hans Urs von Balthasar connects the wakefulness of the child at play and the sleeping child through his

---

13   Maitland, S. (2008) *A Book of Silence: A Journey in Search of the Pleasures and Powers of Silence.* London: Granta, pp.11–12.

14   Doja, A. (2014) 'Socializing enchantment: a socio-anthropological approach to infant-directed singing, music education and cultural socialization.' *International Review of the Aesthetics and Sociology of Music,* Vol. 45, No. 1: 115–147.

15   Nancy, *The Fall of Sleep,* p.30.

reading of the work of Thérèse.[16] These two activities, play and sleep, of the Incarnate Word fascinated Thérèse, 'who like a real mother was constantly drawn to the divine Child in wonder and reflected in quite a sober, practical way about her relation to him'. It is that relationship which the image of Madonna and Child invites, and which Thérèse sought in the face of Jesus Christ. This pursuit of the mutual gaze of the Holy Face, waking and sleeping, is captured in the psalms: '"Come," my heart say, "seek his face!" Your face, Lord, do I seek' (Psalm 27.8). It also is directly connected to sleeping and waking in another verse: 'As for me, I shall behold your face in righteousness; when I awake I shall be satisfied, beholding your likeness' (Psalm 17.15). The vision of the Christian life is union with the Trinity, beholding the Father in the face of Jesus Christ in the power of the Spirit. Therefore to see the Madonna gazing upon her infant child is to glimpse that intimacy and union.

There is a good deal of nostalgia around the sleep of the child. None more so in some of the carols of Christmas that speak of 'The little Lord Jesus asleep on the hay', or 'The little Lord Jesus no crying he makes'. Von Balthasar is rather more direct in his account of the child, and that includes the Christchild:

> Omnipotence asks through the child; it uses the child's irresistibility, the unconscious charm of the child's gestures, in order to gain that which can only be given freely. These charming little tyrants keep adults occupied all the time… Even when they are asleep, one has to be quiet; and when they play, they often take up the whole house, and nothing is safe from them.[17]

So the sleeping child affects the lives of those around them. As Doja suggested above, the lullaby is instrumental in moving the child into sleep, so is not a neutral action. In addition to adoration, attentiveness on the part of the mother is the fruit of a sleeping child. Von Balthasar comments:

> Because the child is asleep, the mother is awake. Because he gives himself freely, the mother is alert and watching. Because he

---

16   Balthasar, H.U. von (1968) *Man in History: A Theological Study.* London: Sheed and Ward, p.252.

17   Balthasar, *Man in History*, p.252.

has apparently broken off contact, the mother redoubles the communication. And when she has to sleep herself, then she must be turned towards the child so that she wakes at its slightest movement. 'I sleep,' says the bride in the Song of Solomon, 'but my heart wakes.' The mother's capacity of attentive readiness has been activated by the child. She has only to open herself to her maternal nature which guides her. Her readiness echoes the helpless dependence of the child. And thus, it is again seen that the divine Child, in becoming man, draws us into his childlikeness by making us mothers.[18]

The sleep of the child engenders attentiveness and adoration on the part of the parent and so sleep becomes relational even in its solitude. The first place in which human beings experience solitude, and sleep, is, paradoxically, in the profoundly relational location of the womb.

O happy sleep

Thérèse reflected on both the playful and the sleeping Christ. The feast of the Nativity of Jesus prompts a reflection in her autobiography *Story of a Soul* in which she writes about a particular Midnight Mass. Her disappointment in not being able to assist at the Mass is overcome by reference to the verse from the Song of Songs cited above (5.2): 'this trial was very great for my faith, but *the one whose heart watches even when he sleeps* made me understand that those whose faith is like that of a mustard seed He grants *miracles* and moves mountains in order to strengthen this faith which is *still small*'.[19] A gesture from her sister, also in the convent, had cheered her, enabling her to meditate further on the sleeping infant Christ:

> ...I returned from Midnight Mass. I found in my room, in the centre of a charming basin, a little boat carrying the Little Jesus asleep with a little ball at His side, and Céline had written these words on the white sail: 'I sleep but my heart watches,' and on the boat itself this one word: 'Abandonment'. Ah! Though Jesus was not yet speaking to His little fiancée [Thérèse], and though His divine eyes

18   Balthasar, *Man in History*, pp.252–253.
19   Thérèse of Lisieux (1996) *Story of a Soul: The Autobiography of Thérèse of Lisieux*, trans. J. Clarke. Washington DC: ICS Publications, p.142. Original italics.

remained closed, He at least revealed himself to her through souls who understood all the delicacies and the love of His Heart.[20]

In a letter to the superior of her convent, Thérèse reflects on the crib and the sleeping Jesus.[21] Thérèse quotes the verse from the Song of Songs (5.2) and says that the sleeping Jesus does not let go of the flowers he was given during the day (a time of wakefulness) and 'His Heart continues dreaming about the happiness of his dear spouse'. Yet the sleep of Jesus, whilst happy, also reveals 'strange objects bearing no resemblance to the springtime flowers. A cross!...a lance!...a crown of thorns!' Thérèse goes on to describe other aspects of Christ's Passion and then: 'He sees the flowers of her [Mother Agnes'] virtues as they scent the sanctuary, and the Child Jesus continues to sleep on peacefully... He awaits the shadows to lengthen...the night of life to give way to the bright day of eternity!'

Visual art has juxtaposed the trustful sleep of the infant with the cross. Christopher Irvine writes about the image of the cross painted in the 1240s by Giunta Pisano now found in the Museum of the Porziuncola:

> I was struck by the serenity of the painted figure of Christ. On this occasion the cross struck me as an image of the 'sleeping Lord', and so I was reminded of the story of how the 'mother of all living' was taken by God from the side of the sleeping Adam in Eden. [This] painted cross...was not intended to evoke the viewer a feeling of sad remorse but to reveal the full extent of God's solidarity with the human predicament and to see this death, the death of Christ, as generative and as opening into a fuller life.[22]

It cannot be known if Thérèse was at all familiar with a genre of painting in which the infant Christ is depicted asleep, reclining on the cross. Exponents of this include Guido Reni (1575–1642), who depicts the infant Jesus sleeping on the cross, and Francisco de la Maza (dates unknown, but active in Valladolid as from 1566), whose

20   Thérèse, *Story of a Soul*, pp.142–143.
21   Thérèse of Lisieux, *Critical Edition of the Complete Works of St Thérèse of Lisieux: General Correspondence, Volume 2, 1890–1897*, trans. J. Clarke (Washington DC: ICS Publications, 1988), pp.838–839.
22   Irvine, C. (2013) *The Cross and Creation in Christian Liturgy and Art*. London: SPCK Alcuin, p.188.

polychrome statue shows the infant Jesus asleep on the cross, which itself rests on a skull. Iconographically the skull represents Adam, the one who tradition says was buried at Golgotha, the Place of the Skull, and who was placed into a deep sleep by God, a sleep out of which Eve was created (itself evoking the pierced side of Christ on the cross).

Thus this adoration of the sleeping infant is full of ambiguity – peaceful sleep and crown of thorns – something captured in a Christmas hymn which bridges the apparent disjunction between the sleeping Christchild and the salvation of the world: 'He sleeps in the manger; he reigns on the throne.'[23] In naïve language Thérèse demonstrates a profound point – how trust is an integral part of adoration, as it is of sleep. Furthermore, she casts the episode of Jesus asleep in the storm in the tranquillity of her meditation, which further expands how the sleep in the stilling of the storm may be read when read through the lens of the Song of Songs.

Sleep and contemplation in mystical writing

There is a double view when we consider the contemplation of the sleeping Christ. On one hand we gaze upon him, and on the other he gazes upon us, as the sleeper. There is a recurrence in the meditations on the sleeping Christ of the verse from the Song of Songs, and it is most pronounced in the monastic mystical tradition from Gregory the Great to Bernard of Clairvaux, amongst others.[24]

Waking sleep: Gregory the Great

In his treatment of sleep, Gregory the Great (540–604) draws on the books Song of Songs and Job, and includes the treatment of sleep. This begins with the restlessness of the Bride and her search through the city for her Lover, which he connects to Mary Magdalene at the tomb. It is in this context that Gregory repeatedly uses Song of Songs 5.2 – 'I sleep but my heart wakes' – to stress, as Grover Zinn puts it, 'the interiorization

---

23 Bramley, H.R. 'The great God of heaven is come down to earth' in *New English Hymnal*, 37.

24 McGinn, B. (1994) *The Growth of Mysticism: From Gregory the Great to the Twelfth Century.* London: SCM Press.

of consciousness in the development of the contemplative discipline'. Gregory understands sleep to be used in three key ways in the Bible that feeds his understanding of contemplation: first, death of the body; second, as negligence; and, third, as 'the peacefulness of life when all carnal desires have been trodden under foot as in the Bride's voice in the Song of Songs, "I sleep but my heart wakes"' (*Moralia* 5.31.54). This third type of sleep is the sleep that had been enjoyed by Jacob at Bethel when 'he closed the eyes of concupiscence (first opened in the Fall), put the stone under his head and slept'. Jacob's vision was made possible, according to Gregory, because the stone on which he rested his head was Christ (*Moralia* 5.31.55). In such a condition, 'Holy men work harder in their sleep than they do when they are awake.' So, McGinn notes, 'the "waking sleep" of Song 5.2 is glossed as the "stillness" of Psalm 46.10, so that Gregory concludes by underlining the message of interiorization':

> Because internal knowledge (*notitia*) is never beheld unless external entanglement ceases, the time of the hidden word and the divine whispering is now rightly expressed in this text, 'In the horror of a vision of the night, when sleep is accustomed to fall upon humans'… The human intellectual soul is lifted high by the engine (*machina*) of its contemplation so that the more it gazes on things higher than itself the more it is filled with terror.[25]

The *notitia* is made possible in the sleep of love. This is because 'external entanglement ceases'. Contemplation is primarily about the relation of love and knowledge. It is surprising at first glance that Gregory introduces the possibility of terror. This terror is suggested in the book of Job (Job 33.15–16) as Elihu rebukes Job. This is not the erotic desire of the restless lover but is, Gregory suggests, the horror of a night vision for Job. This is set in the context of Gregory's exploration of mysticism so that his experience is about the soul stripping away the images of this world that impede it from the ascent. Sleep is stripped away from Job in his distress, anger and angst. Even this time of encounter is denied Job. However, in Gregory's economy, even this deprivation can lead the soul to deeper contemplation since, 'in the silence of the heart, while we keep watch

---

25   McGinn, *The Growth of Mysticism*, p.62.

within through contemplation, we are as if asleep to all things that are without'.[26] Gregory's mystical use of sleep is, unsurprisingly, used both figuratively and literally.

Later mystics have also drawn from the Song of Songs. The restlessness of sleep is accentuated as a way of lying expectantly for the Beloved. Words attributed to Peter Damian (1007–1072) echo the Song of Songs:

> At once I rose from my bed,
> ran to lift the latch.[27]

Also from the late eleventh century comes the 'Sequence on the Virgins' which uses erotic language to describe the encounter with God. It again recalls the language of the Song of Songs, describing, as McGinn puts it, 'the praise of the "happy nuptials" (*O felices nuptie*), in which Christ sleeps with his virgins in "sweet repose" (*requies dulcis*)':

> In these beds
> Christ sleeps with them:
> Happy the sleep,
> Sweet the rest,
> In which, when she is cherished,
> The loyal maiden,
> Within the embraces
> Of the heavenly Bridegroom,
> With his right arm
> Embracing her as a bride,
> His left arm under her head,
> She falls asleep.
> Wakeful in heart,
> In body she sleeps,
> On the Bridegroom's loving
> Breast she slumbers.[28]

---

26 St Gregory the Great, *Moralia* 30.16.54.
27 McGinn, *The Growth of Mysticism*, p.145.
28 McGinn, *The Growth of Mysticism*, p.145.

It continues:

> Upon their bosom
> He lies at mid-day
> Between their breasts
> He sets his sleeping-place.

This is sleep as relational and intimate. It is expressive of the double gaze of Christ the sleeper and Christ the one who watches over the sleeper.

Vital and wakeful slumber: sleep in Bernard of Clairvaux

In a sermon that relates to the Song of Songs (2.6–7), Bernard explores the embrace in relation to sleep, understanding sleep in Christ's embrace as 'a vital and wakeful slumber illuminating the interior sense (*sensus*), driving away death and giving eternal life. It is truly a sleep that does not dull the interior sense but leads it away (*abducat*). It is also a death.' This 'vital and wakeful slumber' is a death because for Bernard it is 'ecstasy', removing the soul from life's cares in which a 'holy and vehement thought (*cogitatio*)' surpasses customary ways of thinking. Bernard sees this ecstasy as something of contemplation: 'the experience is one of true rest', where 'the soul, overcome by the beauty of the spot, sleeps sweetly in her beloved's embrace, that is, in spiritual ecstasy'. The Song of Songs speaks of the sleep of the Bride (Song of Songs 2.6 and 8.3) and in other Cistercian writings is likened to the *otium quetis* or *sabbati* of the monastic tradition. In that regard sleep is both generative and creative. A prominent theme in Bernard's work is the embrace. This is not the same as lying between the breasts of a virgin but it is, along with the kiss, another of his motifs (much as Adam's sleep in Genesis 2.21): 'do not stir or awaken love until it is ready' (Song of Songs 8.4). Sleep may be likened to a time of gestation, from which prayer breaks in through contemplation.

The nuptial imagery of the Song of Songs is picked up in a German medieval text, *A Teaching of the Loving Knowledge of God*, in which dream-visions feature. McGinn quotes a passage referring to Song of Songs 2.6:

Whenever I sleep, then he leads
My soul, as if in a dream, into the fruitful meadow
Of the Holy Spirit,
And my inner spirit into the brightness
Of heavenly wisdom.
This is the highest bliss
Which someone still in exile can enjoy.
Because it deals with a dark and foreign realm,
This bliss is more a dream than a truth.[29]

The other mystical writer from whom insights can be drawn into early reflections on the relationship between sleep and mysticism is Hugh of St Victor (1096–1141). Hugh, like Gregory and Bernard, draws from the Song of Songs and Job and adds in the book of Revelation. So, he presents three biblical images: the three 'suspensions' found in Job 7.15; the three silences suggested by John (Revelation 8.1); and the three sleeps of Solomon in Song of Songs 5.2. For Hugh the three silences – of mouth, mind and reason – are necessary, 'because of the rapture of the soul in the anointing of an "ineffable joy" in God (*ineffabile gaudium*), which cannot be comprehended'. Hugh's treatise cites 1 Corinthians 6.17 – 'anyone united to the Lord becomes one spirit with him' – and enables the soul to accomplish 'the sleep of the three faculties of the soul (*ratio–memoria–voluntas*)'. This sleep of the three faculties is 'the sleep of heavenly sweetness [which] seizes the full anointed [mind] and then it dissolves and rests in the embrace of the highest light'. Prayer, silence and sleep are integral to the mystical experience.

Bernard of Clairvaux's sermons on the Song of Songs only go as far as the third chapter, so his insights directly on Song of Songs 5.2 are not available. However, the theme of presence and absence – where the Bridegroom is sought and to be found – is picked up in Sermons 75–79, which correspond to Song of Songs 3.1–4. Just as 5.2 speaks of the one who sleeps yet whose heart is awake, Bernard locates his focus on the bed of the one who seeks. This place of sleep has become a place of wakefulness and pursuit. Bernard draws from the Vulgate translation: 'Nightlong on my little bed I sought Him Whom my soul loveth. I will arise and go about the city;

---

29 McGinn, *The Growth of Mysticism*, p.351.

through the streets and squares and I will seek Him Whom my soul
loveth. I sought Him, and I found Him not' (Song of Songs 3.1–2).
The littleness of the bed is key to Bernard's exegesis. This is not the
place to seek him – the bed is inadequate. The littleness of a bed is
not the problem – 'for I remember that He was Himself born as a
Little One for us' – rather it represents the narrowness of the human
pursuit, if not in ardour. Bernard contrasts the necessarily little bed of
the Incarnate Lord in his humanity but the expansiveness of the bed
from which his divinity was begotten:

> Was not the sepulchre a little bed? Was not the manger one? Was not
> the Virgin's womb another? But the Bosom of the Father, whence
> he was begotten, was a great bed, not a little one, and more aptly
> compared to a royal throne than to a bed at all... So the Bride is
> right to say '*my* little bed'; for obviously whatever of our weakness
> there is in God belongs not to His Nature but to ours.[30]

What belongs to human experience in Christ is shared with human
beings now: 'the new-born babe's mortality, the little child's infirmity,
the dying of the Crucified, the slumber of the corpse, all these things
belong to me'. No longer can he be sought there, on the '*little* bed' –
'He is risen, He is not here!' – and so Bernard concludes: 'He will lie
down no more; He sits. Or perhaps I should say He sits to judge and
stands to succour us.' The place of sleep, the bed, induces through
Bernard a more expansive vision of the contemplative pursuit of
the Bridegroom.

   This exploration of sleep and mysticism reveals at best some very
creative, or at worst fanciful, uses of sleep. It is however pertinent
to this exploration in two key ways. First, sleep is an indispensable
means of reflection in mystical thought, drawn as it is from scripture.
Second sleep can be used in a figurative way creatively and almost
inexhaustibly to inform the spiritual life. Yet for all that Bernard and
other Cistercians say about sleep, and its insights into contemplation,
they do allow for sleep to be interrupted, since the Divine Lover
may wake the sleeping bride from the sleep of contemplation, 'to
more useful things (*utiliora*)' such as the desire for good works.
This also reveals the ambiguity of a Christian theology of sleep

---

30   St Bernard, *On the Song of Songs*, 234.

because it explicitly says there are other things more useful than sleep: the sleeping/waking nexus makes for an unresolved and unresolvable tension.

Where am I when I sleep?

The question of who I am when I am asleep is addressed by the mystics and is further opened up by Augustine's questions. This chapter will conclude by considering Rainer Maria Rilke's treatment of sleep and how we might be said to be present in sleep and to what and to whom. We will conclude by drawing these insights together and returning to the sleeping Jesus in whom we can locate a trustful, attentive sleep, such that we can say that the Christological posture is the theosomniac posture par excellence.

Sleep and self-awareness

The way in which a person can be both aware and unaware at the same time appears contradictory, as would the declaration that 'I sleep, but my heart wakes' (Song of Songs 5.2). This is a theological statement which means that having fallen into sleep the sleeper can still pay attention and recollect. Insomnia is not simply the state of being awake, but is the state of a person desiring sleep. The commitment to being awake has gone. It does not mean that insomnia enables someone to say, 'I *wish to sleep*, but my heart wakes.'

Jesus' sleep on the boat is a trustful sleep and is therefore not self-aware but aware of the source of peace and security. To declare 'I will lie down and sleep' demands that we set aside the self-awareness which is destructive. As McGilchrist describes:

> Too much self-awareness destroys not just spontaneity, but the quality that makes things live; the performance of music or dance, of courtship, love and sexual behaviour, humour, artistic creation and religious deviation become mechanical, lifeless, and may grind to a halt if we are too self-aware.[31]

---

31 McGilchrist, I. (2010) *The Master and His Emissary: The Divided Brain and the Making of the Western World.* New Haven and London: Yale University Press, p.180.

Insomnia is an acute self-awareness, an unrequited desire. The gift of sleep diminishes self-awareness, which enables a form of receptivity that is both outside the self and deep within it. Sleep is 'ecstatic' in the sense of *ekstasis*, a coming out of oneself.

Augustine: personality, identity and sleep

It is this very self-awareness that Augustine is acutely aware of and is troubled by. He knows that the self-image projected towards other people cannot be masked before God, and so the time immediately prior to sleep exposes the reality of personal identity in a stark way. That gives the right context for William Downes' suggestive point that 'consciousness as an experiencing self is the evanescent moving point between memory and anticipation'.[32] This is not restricted, in Augustine's mind, to the moments before sleep, but during it as well.

To memory and anticipation we may add recollection as featuring in Augustine's understanding of what happens to him in sleep. It is the recollection of images during sleep, and their vivid character, that raises the question for him of what constitutes his true identity and when that is evident. Augustine speaks of sexual images that 'attack' him. He continues: 'while I am awake they have no force, but in sleep they not only arouse pleasure but even elicit consent, and are very like the actual act'.[33] Augustine connects memory and sleep as images from his pre-baptismal life return to him. There is a stark contrast between how he handles memory awake and asleep. He views sleep as a time when memories 'fixed there by my [sexual] habit' can come back. This is an 'illusory image' that affects his flesh with great force and have an effect 'which the reality could not have when I am awake'. He echoes the psalms: 'Yea, even like as a dream when one awaketh: so shalt thou make their image to vanish out of the city' (Psalm 73.19). The vulnerability of identity is highlighted in relation to sleep because of the unknowing associated with it. Augustine's anxiety hinges on human identity because it raises questions about his true self and his intentionality: 'during this time of sleep surely it is not my true self, Lord my God? Yet how great a difference between

---

32   Williams, R. (2014) *The Edge of Words: God and the Habits of Language*. London: Bloomsbury, p.75.

33   Augustine, *Confessions* X.xxx (41), 203.

myself at the time when I am asleep and myself when I return to the waking state.'

Paradoxically sleep both masks and unmasks true identity. In *Christian Devotion* Baillie describes this focused masking of identity immediately prior to sleep: 'very often, I fear, our thoughts upon our beds are definitely harmful, or definitely shameful. They are such as we would not let other people know for all the world.' There is an opportunity with the falling of sleep to mask and bury the inconveniences and inconsistencies of an externally projected self-image. As Baillie goes on to comment, 'they may not always be mean and base, but they are usually – oh, so trivial'. The question of the 'real me' is heightened by the intrusion of personal shame.

Augustine is asking, in effect, which is my true face: my waking face or my sleeping face? That question probes the relationship between the waking and sleeping life. Is it, as Baillie suggests, that 'if there were no evil in our waking souls there would be no evil in our dreams'? To ask that question is in itself disquieting, but for Augustine this throws into sharper focus the question of how rationality fits into this. If he does not know his true self when asleep, then what of his other faculties? 'Surely,' he says, 'reason does not shut down as the eyes close'. His conclusion is that reason 'cannot fall asleep with the bodily senses', because if that were so, how can he act when he does not give assent to his actions? And so there are times when 'often in sleep we resist'. Augustine wants to maintain his ability, in some way, to act rationally, and in accordance with what is required by chastity. Nancy's observation articulates Augustine's fear:

> Now, you say, doesn't thinking fall asleep and give way to fantasies. Don't think it for a second. Though it remains true – painfully true – that the sleep of reason gives birth to monsters, it is no less true that it is by letting itself be inclined to sleep, to dream, and to the possibility of no longer waking that thought lets itself awaken to the last possible day of its full probity: the first day, the day without day of our holy eternity.[34]

Augustine uses sleep as a reference point to discuss 'occurrences and our will' and to acknowledge there are times when 'we did not actively

---

34 Nancy, *The Fall of Sleep*, p.45.

do what, to our regret, has somehow been done in us'. This is the loss of control he knows when and which cannot be held in check when asleep. So he asks whether his conscience is polluted by a sleeping, involuntary, act. And if he is not in control of that act, then who is? As he says, 'it cannot be the case, almighty God, that your hand is not strong enough to cure all the sickness of my soul and, by a more abundant outflow of your grace, to extinguish the lascivious impulses of my sleep'. Augustine wrestles with this question of identity through sleep because it is a focus of 'the wide gulf between the occurrences and our will'. Sleep highlights very forcibly the issue the apostle Paul describes in Romans about doing that which he does not want to do (Romans 7.15–25).

Augustine's dilemma is echoed, but contradicted, by Browne, who writes: 'For my waked judgement discontents me, ever whispering unto me that I am from my friend; but in my friendly dreams in the night requite me, and make me think I am within his arms.' Browne suggests that in some way all are asleep in this world, and that the 'conceits of this life are as mere dreams to those of the next, as the phantasms of the night to the conceits of the day'. Browne's is a more optimistic view of sleep and human nature:

> We are somewhat more than ourselves in our sleeps, and the slumber of the body seems to be but the waking of the soul. It is the ligation of sense, but the liberty of reason; our waking conceptions do not match the fancies of our sleeps.[35]

It is important to note that Augustine is not unremittingly suspicious of sleep. Sleep is more of an unknown land to him in which he, even as a regular inhabitant, is not yet at home. He is far more at ease about sleep in understanding it in relation to the repose that God gives. Repose is a gift of God that is to be found in God.[36] In support of this notion he cites the psalmist: 'I will go to sleep and have my dream' (Psalm 4.9). Sleep is a relief from toil because God's repose 'forgets all toil'. Anything less than God cannot provide the 'rest of contentment' even to itself.[37] It is only God who can 'lighten our darkness (Psalm 17.29)…and our darkness will become as midday

---

35   Browne, T., ed. Winney, J. (1963) *Religio Medici*, 91.
36   Augustine, *Confessions* IX.iv (11). Cambridge: Cambridge University Press, p.162.
37   *Confessions* XIII.viii (9), 277.

(Isaiah 58.10)'. In this Augustine also addresses the relationship between God's Sabbath and sleep. He does this by referring to the 'peace of quietness, the peace of sabbath, a peace with no evening (2 Thessalonians 3.16)'. What will pass is the rhythm of the creation of each day in which there is 'both morning and evening'. Human beings need rest and sleep at the end of each day, but God does not. Indeed, for Augustine, 'the seventh day has no evening and has no ending. You [Lord] sanctified it to abide everlastingly.'[38] The final repose is when 'we may also rest in you for the Sabbath of eternal life', thus linking sleep, Sabbath, rest and death. God embraces rest and sleep:

> There also you will rest in us, just as now you work in us. Your rest will be through us, just as now your works are done through us. But you, Lord, are always working and always at rest. Your seeing is not in time, your movement is not in time, and your rest is not in time. Yet your acting causes us to see things in time, time itself, and the repose which is outside time.[39]

Because God's rest is his own rest, he has no need neither to slumber nor sleep, unlike his creatures whilst they are alive.

Sleep as a place and a time

The term 'thin places' has gained increasing currency as describing places where God's presence seems particularly vivid, as if the perceived boundary between heaven and earth is thin and therefore more porous. This is a spatial concept. Sleep should not be seen in simply spatial terms, but in temporal terms too. So the spatial 'thin place' can be reworked as a temporal concept, as 'thin *time*'. If this is so, then sleep is a time that offers a way of being that is more receptive to God. Jacob's dream at Bethel combines both the thin place and the thin time concepts. On waking from sleep Jacob contemplates the place as much as the experience of sleep: 'How awesome is this place! This is none other than the house of God, and this is the gate of heaven' (Genesis 28.17).

---

38 *Confessions* XII.xxxvi (50), 304.
39 *Confessions* XII.xxxvii (52), 304.

Jacob understands this theophany spatially and located in a particular place, but it also takes place temporally, during sleep, which also makes his sleeping a thin time. Rainer Maria Rilke (1875–1926) catches the sense of the thin time in *Prayers of a Young Poet* as he writes:

> Even when I sleep I am awake.
> Sunk in the hems of your senses,
> I hear Your dreams like winds
> and willing like the trees I speak
> to You many syllables and strange.[40]

Mark Burrows describes these verses, and the ones that precede them, as a 'posture of watching that expresses a long and patient waiting, the kind of attentiveness inherent in the work of prayer'. Sleep is a liminal, thin time, and often features in Rilke's poems along with darkness and night. This darkness, and the sleep associated with it, is not a place of fear. Burrows suggests that, for Rilke, 'darkness is the place of God's becoming, the heart of the divine and the source of spiritual fecundity'. Moreover, God is one who is always becoming, the 'dawning one from whom the morning rose'. So, God is 'the darkness from which [we] come'. Thus Rilke takes us into God in a mode of being and thinking that is unfamiliar and strange to many, and yet that is paradoxically a universal experience, as is sleep. Burrows suggests that Rilke has '[the] conviction that "dark hours" are a source of life, and that the "night" becomes the cradle of artistic and spiritual generativity' and that this shapes his poems throughout. The thin place, or time, of poetry is one where God can seem very close and vivid, and also unfamiliar and strange.

Why might a particular place like the ruins of a monastery on a craggy moor be any more a place where God will intrude into daily life, or why might a time of prayer be any more the time when we are most consciously alert to God? The answer is perhaps that the thinness of the place or moment is affecting for the person, and not for God. Relating this to sleep as a thin time, it is the question that is seen in Augustine who asks when he is most truly *himself* – is it when

---

40   Rilke, R.M. (2013) *Prayers of a Young Poet*, trans. Burrows M. Brewster, MA: Paraclete Press, p.96.

he is awake or asleep? Likewise in a different, but complementary, way, Rilke gives an intense, and not easy, way of reflecting on our 'here-ness' (*Da-sein*), our senses and our finitude. This chimes with the experience of sleep and prayer, in which there is a recognition of 'a second life, timeless and wide'. Burrows quotes Gaston Bachelard in saying that the place of 'non-knowing [is] not a form of ignorance but a difficult transcendence of knowledge'. This is a really significant point connecting recollecting bodies in sleep and the life of prayer: neither is a form of ignorance, as some might suggest, but both are 'a difficult transcendence of knowledge'.

The 'here-ness' of sleep is found in the psalms. Ekirch suggests, from a wide range of references in the literature, that until the close of the modern era Western Europeans on most evenings experienced 'not one but two major intervals of sleep, bridged by up to an hour or more of quiet wakefulness'. This predates our own consolidated sleep. Ekirch suggests that this break in sleep was used in various ways: urinating; conversing; 'intimate relations'; and praying. This may be the time in which the psalmist envisaged that 'when I think of you on my bed, and meditate on you in the watches of the night' (Psalm 63.6), 'I commune with my heart in the night; I meditate and search my spirit' (Psalm 77.6). John Climacus recognises the power of such recollection before sleep: 'It can happen that our meditation on the psalms may persist even into our time of sleeping...the soul endlessly preoccupied with the word of God will love to be preoccupied by it in sleep too.' In this way the sleeper, paradoxically, begins to be awake to God even when asleep because they have become present to God even as they sleep.

3

BE SOBER, BE VIGILANT

Sleep is a gift from God: God gives his beloved sleep. However, there are times when a sacrificial approach to the gift is necessary. This is most evident in the motif of the sentinel and lookout; the one who eschews sleep and watches on behalf of the community: this is all about vigilance. The theme of vigilance begins to move our focus from falling asleep and who we are when we are asleep into juxtaposing sleep with its repudiation. Vigilance makes sense as a counterpoint to sleep. This is a further outworking of the theosomniac motif 'I sleep, yet my heart wakes'.

Vigilance comes out of sleep, but we can fail to be vigilant even when we are awake. So in this sense sleep is a foil to the theological imperative to watchfulness and attention either to sound the alarm or proclaim that 'the Bridegroom is here'.

The Christian practice that maps this theological motif is not Compline but Vigils. Vigils draw from the parables and are enacted particularly in early Christian and monastic practice. In contemporary usage the secular vigil has become a gathering at a traumatic time rather than the interruption of sleep so as to watch expectantly. Many people practise vigils in the latter sense when they are not aware of it; for example, it is at midnight that many people herald the birth of Christ at Christmas. At the very time when it would be expected that people should be deeply at sleep, they are awake, alert and expectant, hearts filled with joy celebrating again the coming of the Saviour, the Bridegroom.

The watchful life

Although they demand the end of a period of sleep, vigils are not unremittingly negative about it. They do contrast the characteristics and benefits of sleep with the need to be alert, to watch and pray. Vigils, like Compline, are a habit and habitation of the Spirit: this is why sleep, and needful rest, is deliberately intruded into.

The merits and provenance of the practice of vigils are not uncontested. Richard Foster describes the spiritual discipline of what he calls 'watchings'. This term comes from the Authorised Version reference to Paul's watching during his hardships. The NRSV refers to 'sleepless nights', which implies an enforced sleeplessness rather than the proactive watching of the vigil. Foster defines 'watching' as 'abstaining from sleep in order to attend to prayer or other spiritual duties'. Whilst Foster is ambivalent about watchings and vigils, there is scriptural precedent. As well as Paul being awake and praying during the time when he is in prison, Jesus rises early in the morning to go and pray (Mark 1.35), thereby setting a pattern for vigils. And he prays into the night in the Garden of Gethsemane. The vigil of Maundy Thursday is the defining vigil of the Church. It places contemporary disciples with Christ in his intercession to the Father. One writer has said that 'a Christian account of the "experiences that matter most" should be derived from a consideration of the ways in which Jesus came to bear the responsibility of his mission and, especially, of how it went with him in Gethsemane'. There Jesus deliberately stays awake to place himself in the posture of attention to the Father. This is in dramatic contrast to the sleeping disciples.

In relation to sleep, vigils have a place in the life of the Church drawn primarily, as suggested, from the Triduum. This is evident in monastic and contemplative practice. As a Liturgical Hour Vigil moves from darkness into light, it draws deeply from the 'vigil' of creation, the *fiat lux*. Being watchful in darkness is one of the tasks of sleep, but also of the one awakening in the *hypnopompia*, the movement towards wakefulness. Vigils is a liminal hour touching night and day, darkness and light, waking and sleeping. It was at dawn that Mary Magdalene came to the tomb of Jesus in her vigil; at dawn when Jacob, having wrestled through the night with the angel, received the blessing. For David Steindl-Rast the hour is also 'a symbol of the waking up we have to do in the midst of our lives… this watching in the night and waiting for the light, this wakefulness, is a forceful reminder to wake up throughout the day from the world of sleep to another reality'.

Vigilance and watchfulness

The theme of vigilance, and the need to be alert, runs through the Gospels, especially the Synoptic Gospels, and into Paul's letters too. This vigilance has an eschatological imperative to it and is often bound up in apocalyptic passages. Vigilance is also clearly and insistently used by Jesus to characterise a true disciple. To be vigilant is to be alert and attentive, even in times when it is hard, for example when someone is traumatised (as were the disciples in Gethsemane), under threat or when it is night and sleep is weighing heavily.

What differentiates waking watchfulness and vigilance from insomnia? This may seem a somewhat brutal or pastorally insensitive question. Emmanuel Levinas suggests: 'Insomnia is constituted by the consciousness that it will never finish, that is, that there is no longer any way of withdrawing from the vigilance to which one is held, Vigilance without end.' Following Levinas, Simon Morgan Wortham suggests that at the point of consciousness's capacity to sleep the 'ego' 'is confronted by the radical vigilance of insomnia'.

However, if vigilance is conflated with insomnia, then by implication vigilance is cast as an affliction, such that vigilance is not sought, but is forced upon the would-be sleeper. Maurice Blanchot (1907–2003) suggests:

> Insomnia, wakefulness or vigilance, far from being definable as the simple negation of the natural phenomenon of sleep, belongs to the categorical antecedent to all anthropological attention and stupor. Ever on the verge of awakening, sleep communicates with vigilance; while trying to escape, sleep stays tuned in, in an obedience to the wakefulness which threatens it and calls to it, which demands.[1]

In contrast, McGilchrist sees the task of vigilance as being responsive to the world around us, not simply as a restlessness or wakefulness:

> Alertness and sustained attention may have the ring of technical 'functions', just the sort of things it's hard to get excited about outside the psychology lab. But, like vigilance, they are the ground of our being in the world, not only at the lowest, vegetative level, but at the highest, spiritual levels ('Brethren, be sober, be vigilant', O Mensch,

---

1   Morgan Wortham, S. (2013) *The Poetics of Sleep: From Aristotle to Nancy*. London: Bloomsbury, p.104.

'gib acht!'). Without alertness, we are as if asleep, unresponsive to the world around us; without sustained attention, the world fragments; without vigilance we cannot become aware of anything we do not already know.[2]

Sustained attention is, as McGilchrist suggests, against the fragmentary pressures of the world. Indeed, the dis-memberment of the world is countered by the re-membering of vigilance. In that way vigilance has a eucharistic character. As the disciples left the Last Supper their commission was to be vigilant, as is the commission of each disciple at the end of the Eucharist. Going in the peace of Christ is the commission to sustained attention to the world in which the Church is vigilant and expectant.

Vigilance is not just about becoming aware of things that were not already known, although it certainly includes that. Rather, theologically, vigilance is grounded in expectant longing both for what is promised, something expected and, as the parables show, that which is unexpected. Vigilance goes even further into an unknowing of what is to come and is not simply about the accumulation of knowledge. Vigilance is about being present, watching when there is nothing yet to see. For the Christian disciple alertness is about being responsive both to the world and to the ways of the Kingdom of God. Jesus' calls to vigilance are typically set within, or are the point of, parables of the Kingdom.

Wise and foolish bridesmaids: Matthew 25.1–13

The parables of watchfulness end with the injunction 'keep awake therefore'. The parable of the ten bridesmaids falls into that category with expectancy rooted in the role of the bridesmaid to herald the coming of the bridegroom. All ten bridesmaids 'became drowsy and slept' (Matthew 25.5) because of the delayed arrival of the bridegroom. It is important to note that the wisdom of the wise bridesmaids is not that they did not sleep at all. Rather, they sleep ready and prepared. The bridesmaids themselves are not the sentinels but are those who respond to the sentinel's call. Someone else is staying awake on

---

2   McGilchrist, I. (2010) *The Master and His Emissary: The Divided Brain and the Making of the Western World.* New Haven and London: Yale University Press.

their behalf. The sentinel calls at midnight and all wake. The sleep is used to highlight the lack of expectancy of the foolish.

The difference between the wise and foolish is that the quality of their sleep is different: 'I sleep, yet my heart wakes' (Song of Songs 5.2). The expectancy of the wise is also shown in the way in which they have prepared for the falling of sleep. They were ready for the onset of sleep by having considered their waking. In the context of practical wisdom the Book of Proverbs reflects the relationship between sleep and wise acting: 'a child who gathers in summer is prudent, but a child who sleeps in harvest brings a shame' (Proverbs 10.3).

The response in hymnody to the parable alights on the central place of sleep and the expectancy of the wise bridesmaids. In 'Wake, O wake! with tidings thrilling', Philipp Nicolai (1556–1608) captures the moment of the cry that goes up at the moment when the bridegroom comes (Matthew 25.6).

> Wake, O wake! with tidings thrilling
> The watchmen all the air are filling,
>   Arise, Jerusalem, arise!
> Midnight strikes no more delaying,
> 'The hour has come!' we hear them saying.
> Where are ye all, ye virgins wise?
> The Bridegroom comes in sight,
> Raise high your torches bright!
>   Alleluya!
> The wedding song
> Swells loud and strong:
> Go forth and join the festal throng.[3]

A fifth-century Greek hymn, 'Behold the Bridegroom cometh', is far more negative about sleep. It particularly has in mind those who are like the foolish bridesmaids who sleep unprepared: '…woe to that dull servant, whom the Master shall surprise / with lamp untrimmed, unburning, and with slumber in his eyes.' The hymn defaults to negativity about sleep and less about unpreparedness. In regard to sleep it says:

---

3   *New English Hymnal (NEH)* 16.

> Do thou, my soul, beware, lest thou in sleep sink down,
> Lest thou be given o'er to death, and lose the golden crown;
> But see that thou be sober, with a watchful eye, and thus
> Cry – Holy, holy, holy God have mercy upon us.

And in similar vein:

> Beware, my soul; beware, beware, lest thou in slumber lie,
> And, like the Five, remain without, and knock and vainly cry;
> But watch, and bear thy lamp undimmed, and Christ shall gird thee on,
> His own bright wedding-robe of light – the glory of the Son.[4]

Lawrence Tuttiett (1825–1897) has a very gloomy (his word) account of sleep and night, but also introduces the Advent prayer imperative 'Come', as in '"Surely I am coming soon". Amen. Come Lord Jesus' (Revelation 22.20):

> O quickly come, sure Light of all,
> For gloomy night broods o'er our way,
> And weakly souls begin to fall
> With weary watching for the day:
> O quickly come; for round thy throne
> No eye is blind, no night is known.[5]

Sleep, in this account, is weakness and the inability to stay awake and alert. Even his vigilance is cast as 'weary watching'.

This theme is highly persistent. Another ancient hymn, this time Latin, *Conditor alme siderum*, evokes the night, and its stars, into which the eternal Word comes. It speaks of a world drawing into evening-tide, a world that, as Stanley Hauerwas argues, is slipping into the numbness of a sleep evacuated of hope. This sentiment is echoed in Joseph Antice's (1808–1836) hymn, 'When came in flesh the incarnate Word, / The heedless world slept on.' It is to another Latin hymn, *Vox clara ecce intonate*, drawing on Matthew 25.1–13, that more sparkle is given to the sleep of the bridesmaids:

---

4   *EH* 3.
5   *NEH* 13.

> Hark! A herald voice is calling:
> 'Christ is nigh,' it seems to say;
> 'Cast away the dreams of darkness,
> O ye children of the day!'
>
> Startled at the solemn warning,
> Let the earth-bound soul arise;
> Christ her Sun, all sloth dispelling,
> Shines upon her morning skies.[6]

In the midst of legitimate, but negative, readings of Matthew 25.1–13, a more optimistic note should be struck. The theosomniac reading concedes that all were asleep; enjoying the gift that God gives. However, the key element to draw from the parable is the nature of expectation and anticipation in preparing for sleep that is ready to be awake and alert. The overwhelming factor is joyful anticipation that the Bridegroom will come. The unexpected timing of the Bridegroom's arrival heightens its impact.

Time to wake from sleep

In Stanley Hauerwas' characterisation of a sleepy world, the calling of the Christian disciples is to be the lookout and sentinel who both sounds the warning and also heralds the arrival of Christ the Bridegroom. And if not the lookout then the wise one who is ready to wake alert, expectant and hope-filled since the disciple sleeps alert.

There is a desperate sense of urgency to this in Paul's letter to the Romans: 'Besides this, you know what time it is, how it is now the moment for you to wake out of sleep. For salvation is nearer to us now than when we became believers; the night is far gone and the day is near' (Romans 13.11–12). Paul's urgent appeal was to sleepy Christians. God's world needs disciples to be awake to him, to be lookouts for the world pointing out the signs of the Kingdom and being signs of the Kingdom. The Church is called to wake the world up to be prepared to receive the light and hope and love of God with lamps prepared and trimmed wicks ready to ignite and set hearts aflame. One does not know the day or time.

---

6   *NEH* 5.

Vigilance derives from not knowing, but also from expecting. It is because the disciple does not know that he or she must be vigilant and awake but also because he or she is expectant. The refrain in these parables is repeatedly 'Therefore keep awake'. Tom Wright sees Matthew 24.36–44 (below), a parable of the necessity for watchfulness, very much in terms of preparation and sets this within the possibility of either the *parousia*, the royal appearing of Jesus himself, or the warning to Christians to be ready for their own death. The passage juxtaposes sleep with the imperative to 'keep awake' (v.42).

> Jesus said, 'But about that day and hour no one knows, neither the angels of heaven, nor the Son, but only the Father. For as the days of Noah were, so will be the coming of the Son of Man. For as in those days before the flood they were eating and drinking, marrying and giving in marriage, until the day Noah entered the ark, and they knew nothing until the flood came and swept them all away, so too will be the coming of the Son of Man. Then two will be in the field; one will be taken and one will be left. Two women will be grinding meal together; one will be taken and one will be left. Keep awake therefore, for you do not know on what day your Lord is coming. But understand this: if the owner of the house had known in what part of the night the thief was coming, he would have stayed awake and would not have let his house be broken into. Therefore you also must be ready, for the Son of Man is coming at an unexpected hour. (Matthew 24.36–44)

Jesus is most anxious to convey to his disciples that his followers must stay awake, like people who know there are going to be surprise visitors coming sooner or later but who don't know exactly when. Commenting on the same passage, Hauerwas concurs:

> The disciples' task is to stay awake, to be ready, exactly because they do not and cannot know the day and hour of the triumph of the Son of Man. Disciples are not in the game of prediction. Rather, they are called to be ready and prepared.[7]

That demands intentional waking, thereby disrupting sleep, since not knowing the time is essential to waking and watching and the

---

7   Hauerwas, S. (2006) *Matthew*. London: SCM Press, p.206.

point of the burglar illustration. Therein lies one of the roots of the Christian practice of vigils. Unlike the parable of the wise and foolish bridesmaids (Matthew 25.1–13), this passage suggests that sleep followed by vigilant waking is not sufficient.

For Hauerwas, 'apocalyptic names the time of waiting'. This kind of waiting is made possible by hope. Sleeping is not waiting without intent and wiling away the time: in the Gospels sleep is the attentive, expectant yet waiting sleep of hope. The notion of hope-filled sleep signals one of Hauerwas' themes in which disciples are shaped and formed, both in their faith and ethical acting, by the habits and practices of the Church. Disciplines of the Church, such as Compline and Vigils, are habit-forming practices around preparation for sleep and on waking from sleep, both ancient and contemporary, much as the wise bridesmaids prepared for sleep knowing their hearts could be awake. The conclusion Hauerwas draws from this Gospel passage, contrasting the Christian disciple with the rest of humanity, is that 'disciples of Jesus must learn how to take the time patiently to hope in a world that thinks it has no time for either hope or patience'.

Weeds among the wheat: Matthew 13.24–30

The thrust of the parable of weeds among the wheat is about the harvest and judgement. When good seed had been sown in the field, 'an enemy came and sowed weeds among the wheat, and then went away' (Matthew 13.25). This happened 'while everybody was asleep'. Vigilance also has a 'slow-burn'; something may only be noticed some time after the sleeper has woken. This is not unlike Saul's realisation after waking from his deep sleep that his enemy in the form of David had raised his camp (1 Samuel 26.6–12). The realisation that weeds had been sown by an enemy in amongst the previously sown good seeds took a long time to wake up to as the seeds germinated and sprouted. This heightens Christian rhetoric around sleep, exemplified by Wright: 'it's up to each church and each individual Christian, to answer the question: are you ready? Are you awake?'

In his treatment of this parable Maurice Nicholl focuses on the phrase 'while men slept', *katheudein tous anthropous*, which the *New Revised Standard Version* renders 'while everybody was asleep' (Matthew 13.25). The 'sleep of men' for Nicholl is that human beings 'cannot keep awake to the full meaning of the teaching given them', just as those who slept whilst the enemy came and sowed weeds, with the weeds representing the contamination of the original teaching. This prompts the need to be awake and to watch. For Nicholl, the parable is about 'the contamination of right understanding by wrong understanding'. The 'sleep of men' is the field, as it were, in which the weeds are sown; the condition of wakefulness is the awareness of the good wheat that is sown in human lives: truth mixes with falsity. This parable gives material from which the Church draws in the prayers for protection from the Evil One before and during sleep.

The coming of the Son of Man: Mark 13.24–37

As noted above, it is not just Matthew who uses the refrain, 'stay awake'; Mark also uses it. The prelude to that declaration is very obviously apocalyptic, but hints at the technical theological sense of apocalyptic as the unveiling of another world made present in this, but also in the popular sense and a dramatic and vivid collapsing world order.

> But in those days, after that suffering, the sun will be darkened, and the moon will not give its light, and the stars will be falling from heaven, and the powers in the heavens will be shaken. Then they will see 'the Son of Man coming in clouds' with great power and glory. Then he will send out the angels, and gather his elect from the four winds, from the ends of the earth to the ends of heaven. (Mark 13.24–27)

The passage opens with a description of the night sky as one turns to sleep; the setting sun signals that sleep is imminent. However, the vision continues, and as the disruption begins, the moon, which for much of the lunar cycle will give some light, is now dark, thus proving that it is not simply that the sun is dark because we can no longer see it, but that the sun is truly darkened because now the moon which of itself has no light cannot even reflect its light. So this is not an ordinary night in which to slumber. Furthermore, stars fall from the heavens.

There is an intriguing connection when Abraham (at this point still named Abram) is brought by God into a covenant relationship by showing him the stars and says, 'Look towards the heaven and count the stars, if you are able to count them. Then he said to him, "So shall your descendants be"' (Genesis 15.5b). Abraham makes sacrifice to the Lord (Genesis 15.7–11) and then, 'As the sun was going down, a deep sleep fell upon Abram, and a deep terrifying darkness descended upon him' (Genesis 15.12). The apocalyptic vision connects the Abrahamic covenant with an episode of sleep which in the Gospel passage also refers to sleep. The observation of nature – in this case the fig tree – asleep, or hibernating, in winter is a hopeful image because it implies the waking of spring or summer. The stars will fall from the heavens just as leaves will fall from the tree, and this is good and also reflects God's faithful covenant promise, illustrated in Abram's sleep, even though it holds trials and tribulations.

'Let us not sleep like others do': 1 Thessalonians

Paul links inattentiveness to sleep in 1 Thessalonians. He equates it with darkness. When the believer is inattentive, it is in the darkness: 'the day of the Lord will come like a thief in the night' (1 Thessalonians 5.2). Neither is to be missed if we know what is good for us. Sleep is not something that those living in Christ should do: 'Let us not fall asleep as others do, but let us keep awake and be sober; for those who sleep sleep at night, and those who are drunk get drunk at night' (1 Thessalonians 5.6). However, as if to acknowledge the biological and psychological need and benefit of sleep and, more importantly, to emphasise the metaphor, Paul concedes that, such is the magnitude of Christ's saving death, 'whether we are awake or asleep we may live with him' (1 Thessalonians 5.10). Those who are awake are the ones who will 'put on the Lord Jesus Christ' who make no provision for the life of the Old Adam, who in one sense is the one who sleeps.

The sentinel

As we have seen, vigilance is a key theme of the New Testament and in Christian life. So what of the sentinel, the lookout, the watchman? The role is highly significant as the one who deliberately eschews sleep on behalf of a community: in the Church of England this role is entrusted to the ministry of priesthood, as reflected in the Ordinal. This draws on the theme of vigilance in the Hebrew Scriptures (Ezekiel 3.17 and 33.7). The texts describe the sentinel as the one who will warn the people, who by definition have not themselves been watching vigilantly.

The refusal of sleep by the sentinel enables others to sleep safely and peacefully. Of the sentinel's relationship with sleep, Jean-Luc Nancy says, 'The sentinel must struggle against sleep, as does Aeschylus's watchman on the roof, as Christ's companions forget to do. Whoever relinquishes vigilance relinquishes attention and intention, every kind of tension and anticipation.' There is an anticipatory dimension to the sentinel which itself refuses sleep.

The role of sentinel is often a lonely one, and one that seeks divine strength. Robert Herrick's (1591–1674) poem *His Litany, To the Holy Spirit* captures this:

> When the world doth sigh and weep,
> And the world is drown'd in sleep,
> Yet mine eyes the watch do keep,
>   Sweet Spirit, comfort me.[8]

Ministry and vigilance

The Church of England Ordinal teaches that priests are to be 'watchmen and stewards of the Lord'. Ezekiel is appointed sentinel for the house of Israel, ready to alert sinners to the consequences of their ways. The insistent warning of the sentinel brings home the message of life and death. Like Ezekiel, the prophet Isaiah is appointed lookout himself (Isaiah 21.6), and this lookout is to look and 'announce what he sees', and he is 'to listen, very diligently' (Isaiah 21.6, 7). This watchman calls out, 'Upon a watchtower I stand, O Lord, continually by day, and at my post I am stationed throughout the night' (Isaiah 21.8). Soon afterwards the watchman, the prophet, is asked, '"Sentinel, what of the night? Sentinel, what of the night" The sentinel says: "Morning comes, and also the night"' (Isaiah 21.12). The sentinel is awake and alert and

---

8   Robert Herrick, 'His Litany To the Holy Spirit' in P. Levi (ed.) (1984) *The Penguin Book of Christian Verse*. London: Penguin.

ready to warn. Sleep is problematised when seen alongside the role of the sentinel.

Rowan Williams casts the priest as 'lookout'. Attentiveness is a key attribute of the lookout. Williams sees this theme in the Ordinal. He reimagines the word watchman not simply to avoid gender sensitivities but to add dynamism and vigour to it for a generation for whom the notion of the watchman is remote. Thus, the priest as watchman becomes the lookout. The lookout, literally and metaphorically, is the person in a community who has to stay awake whilst others are enabled to sleep. A lookout needs to be single minded, and also knowing what she or he is looking out for. Pastors, exercising the role of lookout, are then asked in what way they are lookouts for the sleeping Church. That is a significant question for every priest: what in particular are they looking out for in their ministry; are they looking out for the right things; are those things signs of danger, or are they signs to be welcomed; is the priest, as lookout, really awake? Williams says that 'the priest must first of all be free to see'. To be free to see means to be freed from sleep. He notes, as does the Ordinal, how the language of the Hebrew Scriptures about the prophet as watchman (as in Habakkuk and Ezekiel) 'comes into its own' in relation to the lookout:

> The minister who has to tell the Church what and where it is must be free to see what and where it is. The entire point of being on watch is that you have the chance of seeing what others don't – not as a visionary privilege, but as a weighty and sometimes intensely painful responsibility undertaken for the sake of the whole community.[9]

The biblical conviction is that the lookout watches both for the enemy and the signs of the coming Lord. In this resistance of sleep, even if it is enforced, it is undergirded by the notion that God is the one who never sleeps: 'Unless the LORD guards the city, the guard keeps watch in vain' (Psalm 127.1b). In that darkness the Psalmist cries out, 'I wait for the LORD, my soul waits and in his word I hope; my soul

---

9   Williams, R, (2004) 'The Christian Priest Today': lecture on the occasion of the 150th anniversary of Ripon College, Cuddesdon. Accessed 27 June 2013. http://rowanwilliams.archbishopofcanterbury.org/articles.php/2097/the-christian-priest-today-lecture-on-the-occasion-of-the-150th-anniversary-of-ripon-college-cuddesd

waits for the Lord more than those who watch for the morning, more than those who watch for the morning' (Psalm 130.5, 6).

In his commentary *On the Song of Songs* Bernard of Clairvaux praises the watchman, in the form of the preacher, pastor and monk, who watches and prays while others sleep. These are 'the servants of whom the Saviour said, "Blessed are they whom the Lord, when He cometh, shall find watching"':

> What good watchmen they are, who keep watch while we sleep, that they may give account for our souls! What good guardians are they who are wakeful in spirit and pass the night in prayer, who wisely expose the tricks of the enemy, forestall the plots of the ill-disposed, discover their wiles, break their snares, rend their nets and foil their machinations.[10]

Bernard is also mindful that the true watcher over the people is God: 'They keep watch, and they pray at the same time, knowing their own insufficiency and that "except the Lord keep the city, the watchman waketh but in vain".'

Watching in the temple

The practice of 'incubation' in the Temple of Jerusalem and other sanctuaries and of which Psalm 134 is an example, as described in Chapter 1, constitutes a vigilant practice but not to the extent of other examples so far explored. Psalm 132 is an example of vigilance within the sacral setting:

> I will not enter the dwelling of my house,
> Nor get up into my bed,
> I will not grant sleep to my eyes
> Or slumber to my eyelids,
> Until I find a place for the Lord,
> A dwelling for the Mighty One of Jacob. (Psalm 132.3–5)

The context of the Psalm is the ascetic vow made by David not to rest until he had brought the ark from obscurity to a fitting sanctuary.

---

10   Bernard of Clairvaux, St. (1951) *On the Song of Songs (Sermones in Cantica Canticorum).* Translated and edited by A Religious of CSMV. London: Mowbray. p. 239.

The oath is not to enter his own house or to sleep until that task is complete. The vow connects asceticism with the self-imposed deprivation of rest and sleep. John Eaton suggests that whilst this is not recorded in the historical accounts, for instance 2 Samuel 5.6ff, 'it was remembered in worship because of some custom of later kings also to avoid sleep until the commemorative procession was completed'. Eaton says no more about that as a practice but it certainly represents what is recognisable as a vigil. It also has an interesting theological consequence since in the Psalm no mention is made of David or the king concerned finding rest or sleep but, rather, 'the Lord has chosen Zion; he has desired her for his dwelling. This shall be my resting place for ever.' It is not that the Lord will now sleep, but rather it associates sleep, resting and the significance of a sacred place.

Sleep and self-denial

The call of the sentinel suggests a call both to repentance and faithfulness. In terms of the liturgical year of the Church there is a distinctly Advent and Lenten character to the sentinel. As has been seen in some of the hymnody used, the Advent character is that of being alert to the coming of the bridegroom, awake and expectant, having shaken off sleep.

Lent is the season when Christians are bidden to 'self-examination and repentance; by prayer, fasting, and self-denial; and by reading and meditating upon God's holy word'. This call comes in the context of the need to 'take to heart the call to repentance and the assurance of forgiveness proclaimed in the gospel, and so grow in faith and in devotion to our Lord'. The piety of Lent takes this further. It emphasises self-denial, physical deprivation and hardship, and can be seen in Paul's references in 2 Corinthians in which he refers to sleepless nights along with beatings, imprisonments, hunger and hardship. The *Rule of St Benedict* makes this connection, saying that 'the life of a monk ought to be a continuous Lent'.[11] Echoing Paul's description, Benedict goes on to suggest that 'let each one deny himself some food, drink, sleep…' The juxtaposition between denial of sleep and wakefulness to Christ is at work here.

---

11 *Rule of St Benedict*, 49.1.

Again hymnody articulates some of the themes around sleep, and here in relation to Lent. The sixth-century Latin hymn *Christe qui lux es et dies* takes the themes of light and darkness and picks up familiar themes about Christ keeping watch over the sleeping Christian:

> O Christ, who art the Light and Day,
> Thou drivest darksome night away!
> We know thee as the Light of light,
> Illuminating mortal sight.
>
> All-holy Lord, we pray to thee,
> Keep us to-night from danger free;
> Grant us, dear Lord, in thee to rest,
> So be our sleep in quiet blest.
>
> And while the eyes soft slumber take,
> Still be the heart to thee awake;
> Be thy right hand upheld above
> They servants resting in thy love.

As it continues, the hymn reveals its Lenten context and the re-statement of the graced nature of sleep as a time when God watches over the disciple, as he watched over his Son in the wilderness. Unlike Jesus he watches over us because of our weakness:

> Remember us, dear Lord, we pray
> While in this mortal flesh we stay:
> 'Tis thou who dost the soul defend –
> Be present with us to the end.

The associations of weakness and sleep become prevalent in Lenten hymnody. Using the key phrase 'watch and pray' to associate with sleep, Isaac Williams (1802–1865) weaves together sleep, weakness and God's watchfulness:

> Still ever let me watch and pray,
> And feel that I am frail;
> That if the tempter cross my way,
> Yet he may not prevail.

J.M. Neale (1818–1866) also draws weariness into his Lenten hymn:

> Well I know thy trouble,
> O my servant true;
> Thou art very weary –
> I was weary too;
> But that toil shall make thee
> Some day all mine own,
> And the end of sorrow
> Shall be near my throne.

The weariness, and associated sleep, of the disciple is not something suffered in isolation. A positive appraisal of sleep in the Christian life would want to suggest that sleep is not something to be suffered; rather, sleeplessness is where suffering comes in. Christ shares the weariness of the disciple and the world. So then, sleep is a hallowing and redeeming aspect of Incarnation, even if that is not comfortable: 'stones thy pillow, earth thy bed'. Jesus' invitation to his disciples is to find rest in him (Matthew 11.28–30). The text does not name sleep per se but reveals solidarity with a burdened humanity through the gift of deep rest, a rest that transcends the rest that human beings can achieve by themselves or through their own efforts.

Sleep and self-denial: Bede's Life of St Cuthbert

The *Life of St Cuthbert* by Bede (672–735) details many elements of the saint's life, some of which enter the realms of legend and fable, and some of which bear the ring of authenticity. It is most certainly in the genre of hagiography which was intended 'to stress that the saint was a man of God and shared in divine qualities and even in the power of miracles'. It is also known that Bede greatly admired Cuthbert, Aidan and the Irish monks. As far as sleep is concerned, Bede details both miraculous instances and ascetic. Reading them in the context of contemporary sensibilities, some of Cuthbert's exploits in relation to sleep seem extreme and negative about the body in general and sleep in particular. What does come through is Bede's interest in sleep and the way in which Cuthbert's battling with it is used to demonstrate watchfulness and vigilance.

Bede recounts an instance of how Cuthbert and some companions were stranded, 'languishing', on an island following a violent storm: 'Cuthbert, however, did not waste this leisure time in idleness, nor did he merely sleep through. Night after night was spent in prayer.' Bede relates:

> One night when his companions had gone to sleep and he was keeping watch and praying as usual, he suddenly saw light streaming from the skies, breaking the long night's darkness, and the choirs of the heavenly host coming down to earth.[12]

The angels had come to receive the soul of Aidan, not that Cuthbert was aware at the time that Aidan had died. There are echoes, perhaps deliberate, in Bede's account of the shepherds seeing the angelic host at the nativity of Christ. More illuminating in terms of Cuthbert's attitude to sleep is not that he was rejecting the gift of God to his beloved by being the only one staying awake but that he was awake to witness something others missed, and as shepherd, a lookout, it is always necessary that someone is awake whilst others sleep. Cuthbert's own account runs as follows:

> What wretches we are, given up to sleep and sloth so that we never see the glory of those who watch with Christ unceasingly! After so short a vigil what marvels I have seen! The gate of Heaven opened and a band of angels led in the spirit of some holy man.[13]

Bede's *Life* emphasises Cuthbert's vigilance through the denial of sleep: 'He watched, prayed, worked, and read harder than anyone else.'[14]

One of the things Cuthbert is famed for is his connection not only with the ways of heaven and people but with the animal kingdom too. Bede tells of a night when Cuthbert prayed all night in the sea, and on leaving the sea and resting on the beach he was ministered to by otters who 'warmed his feet with their breath, and tried to warm him with their fur'. The encounter with the otters is preceded by what one might call 'sleep fasting':

---

12   Farmer, D.H. (1965/1983) *The Age of Bede*. London: Penguin, p.49.
13   Bede, *Life of St Cuthbert*, 50.
14   Bede, *Life of St Cuthbert*, 53.

[Cuthbert] was in the habit of rising at the dead of night, while everyone else was sleeping, to go out and pray, returning just in time for morning prayers. One night…he went towards the beach beneath the monastery and out into the sea until he was up to his arms and neck in deep water. The splash of the waves accompanied his vigil throughout the dark hours of the night.[15]

It may be that Cuthbert's denial of sleep was because of a loathing of sleep or subjugation of the body, yet he does not appear to have regarded it that way. When he encountered a monk who had been watching him, he asked him, 'Have you been spying on my night's work?' For Cuthbert, denial of sleep was akin to fasting. Both practices are about denial of a gift that God has given to a particular purpose.

Sara Maitland is blunt about these practices of self-denial, suggesting that 'fasting and sleep deprivation, for example, produce some very particular physiological results that have little or nothing to do with holiness as we understand it'. In the context of fasting, which we may extend to sleep, David Brown refers to 'the strangeness of the extreme asceticism that characterized the lives of so many of the Church's saints'. Maitland's concern seems more to be 'eating disorders', but poor sleep hygiene over a prolonged period can be said to fall into the same category. This strangeness of practice was evident in Cuthbert. One of Bede's accounts tells of him fasting for five days using only an onion to relieve his mouth. After five days he had nibbled a third of one onion. Cuthbert may have been aware of the traditions of the Egyptian Desert which set something of a paradigm for the eremitical life. Verna Harrison cites Poemen's account of the practice of St Antony and other desert monks in their rigours and by staying awake at night. In notes to directors and exercitants of the *Spiritual Exercises*, Michael Ivens commends that

it is not a penance to go without the superfluous, the finer quality and more comfortable, but penance begins when we go without what is in itself suitable in the way we sleep. Again, the more this is done the better, as long as the constitution is not harmed and no serious illness results, and provided nothing is retrenched from

---

15   Bede, *Life of St Cuthbert*, 58.

needful sleep, except in order to arrive at a just mean, if we have the bad habit of sleeping too much.[16]

Ivens' approach to sleep, in the spirit of St Ignatius of Loyola, is demanding yet humane. In contemporary church life and spirituality fasting is often associated with subjugation of the body, even if accompanied by prayer, and the conquering of a bodily need. Yet, as Brown comments, fasting was (and is) more than just a physical act. Food, sexual intercourse and sleep have been subject to this 'fasting' or self-denial. Brown believes it would be wrong to think of even the medieval extremes of ascetic as hatred of the body. Timothy Radcliffe suggests that the point of fasting is to appreciate the food one does have rather than punish the body for the food one does not have. The same may be said of sleep. Deprivation of sleep is not to punish oneself, but to enable the self to be thankful for the gift of sleep. In the way that Jesus multiplied food in the wilderness so abundance is powerfully expressed in the context of scarcity, so the intentional creation of scarcity of sleep, sleep deprivation, becomes a means of receiving God's grace.

Bede's *Life of St Cuthbert* is an account of a graced body whose relationship with sleep and the body was deeply ambiguous in many ways to contemporary sensibilities, and was even noteworthy in the exacting standards of his own day. In Cuthbert we see that deprivation of sleep, even though it is a gift, heightens the gratuity of the gift and does not repudiate it. For Bede, 'the sublimity of the saint's earthly was well attested by his numerous miracles', and no further proof of Cuthbert's sanctity was required. Whilst post-mortem miracles are recorded by Bede, more striking is the account of the state of Cuthbert's body when it was exhumed by his erstwhile brethren 11 years after his death. His body was found to be uncorrupted and 'it seemed not dead but sleeping'.

'On Alertness': vigils in The Ladder of Ascent

In *The Ladder of Ascent* John Climacus (c.579–649) writes 'On Alertness' and connects it to the ancient and enduring practice of vigils. His words capture the intention vigilance through eschewing

---

16   Ivens, M. (1998) *Understanding the Spiritual Exercises.* Leominster: Gracewing, p.84.

sleep: 'Let us see now what happens when we stand in prayer during evening or throughout the day and night before God our King.' Climacus describes different sorts of vigil. The common theme is the contrast between sleep and alertness: 'Alertness keeps the mind clean. Somnolence binds the soul.' So he describes different practices:

> Some keep nightlong vigil, their hands raised in prayer like spirits free of every burden. Others sing the Psalms or read, while some out of weakness, bravely fight sleep by working with their hands. Others think constantly of death and try in this way to obtain a contrite heart.[17]

He even offers a hierarchy of vigils, the first and last persevering out of love for God, the second appropriate for a monk, and the third 'the lowliest road'. For Climacus sleep is the antonym of alertness, and the imperative for alertness is prior to that of sleep, saying: 'the alert monk does battle with fornication, but the sleepy one goes to live with it'. Alertness is prized as something which vigils engender at the expense of sleep, so that 'the vigilant monk is a fisher of thoughts, and in the quiet of the night he can easily observe and catch them'.

Climacus has a collection of sayings on alertness which see excessive or long sleep as 'the tyrant sleep...a cunning fiend'. For him sleep can be tool of demons that tricks the monk at every turn: it proposes manual labour instead of vigilant prayer; it will 'attack' beginners in prayer to make them careless; it leads the way into fornication and impure thoughts. Climacus wrestles with sleep as something good and seeks to face it down in vigils: 'How is it, for instance, that when we are living in luxury and abundance we can keep vigil and remain awake, whereas while fasting and wearing ourselves down with toil, we are wretchedly overcome with sleep?' Sleep can be used to punish the body but is also associated with other 'demons', such as that of despondency, which itself can lead to lust, thus weakening the body and 'causes that sleep which brings about pollutions in those practising stillness'.

Climacus represents the tradition that is deeply ambivalent to sleep. This means that sleep for him is something to be resisted

---

17   From the Prologue to the 'Rule of St Benedict.' Luibhied, *The Ladder of Ascent*, p.196.

because it suppresses alertness and vigilance. Sleep is the arena for sin, and so not to be asleep is in one sense to be alert.

Benedict and monastic vigilance

The *Rule of St Benedict* makes clear that watchfulness is required of a monk. The *Rule* is not as unremittingly negative about sleep as in the earlier tradition of Climacus. Benedict sets the tone for his view of watchfulness and its relationship to sleep in his Prologue to the *Rule*, saying: 'Let us get up then, at long last, for the Scriptures rouse us when they say: "*It is high time for us to arise from sleep*" (Romans 13.11). Let us open our eyes to the light that comes from God.' In that statement Benedict captures the broad New Testament approach to sleep, and the application of that theology in the pastoral context of a monastic rule: watchfulness and vigilance that is at the heart of it.

This watchfulness is worked out through the liturgical hours, drawing on the injunction to rise at midnight to pray (following Psalm 119.62). Benedict devotes two chapters of the *Rule* to describing the celebration of the night office through the seasons of the year. The *Rule* shows the influence of John Cassian, who in his *Conferences* urges a vigilant outlook for monks and explains that 'three things keep a wandering mind in place – vigils, meditation, and prayer'.

It is the spirit of watchfulness that shapes the *Rule*'s attitude to sleep and arrangements for it, with Benedict devoting a whole chapter to arrangements for it in the monastery. He prescribes separate beds and bedding provided by the abbot, 'suitable to monastic life'. As may be expected in a monastic community, as opposed to a hermit, 'all are to sleep in one place'. If the size of the community precludes this, they are to sleep in groups of 10 or 20. Sleep in this context is highly social. Esther de Waal suggests that the sociability of Benedictine sleep is not to do with the dangers of immorality but to enable monks 'to rise with the utmost speed and ease'. This is why Benedict says the monks should sleep clothed, girded with belts and cords (although with their knives removed 'lest they cut themselves'!). Sleep is not bad in itself, but it is to be shaken off quickly. In the dormitory the role of the seniors is to 'quietly encourage' those waking, or still sleeping, monks like Frère Jacques, 'for', as the *Rule* says, 'the sleepy like to make excuses'. De Waal comments that monks 'sleep in a state of availability'. This illustrates the Gospel and Pauline imperatives to be alert. That is the virtue of the wise bridesmaids in the parable. The sleeping and waking life of a monk, as conceived by Benedict, has the aim of sleeping in a deep state of availability to God, and waking in a state of availability to God, in prayer.

Gethsemane

The parables of watchfulness and the role of the sentinel all presage the forthcoming watch in the Garden of Gethsemane. This is the most decisive of all vigilant acts. In it Jesus watches and prays through the night such that he is at one with the Father's will. His disciples Peter, James and John are shown through their sleeping to be unable to share in that watchfulness.

There is another scene in which the disciples fail to stay awake. It is the Transfiguration account which is connected to the Gethsemane watch. The Transfiguration account points to the things to be accomplished in Jerusalem through the glorification of Jesus Christ in his Passion (cf. Matthew 17.1–13; Mark 9.2–8; Luke 9.28–36). Peter, James and John are chosen to accompany Jesus up the mountain and witness these things. In an anticipation of Gethsemane, the companions 'are weighed down with sleep' (Luke 9.32). Translation of *diagregpresantes* varies; it could be either 'but since they had stayed awake' or 'but when they were fully awake'. Nicholl points out that as this took place in the daytime then physical or routine sleep is not being described here. The disciples were 'asleep to greater meaning'. He continues:

> And so, blind to Christ's teaching about the Kingdom of Heaven, and asleep to this idea of the transformation of Man, when in the presence of the actual manifestation before them, they were said to be weighted down with sleep. The quality of their minds, their degree of consciousness, their level of understanding, could not reach it.[18]

---

18   Nicholl, M. (1950) *The New Man: An Interpretation of Some Parables and Miracles of Christ.* London: Penguin. p. 127.

The dazzling light of Transfiguration and the awfulness of the Passion closed the eyes of the disciples, eyes that needed opening, as if from sleep. The disciple is called to have open eyes and mind to that glorious revelation of Jesus Christ. In contemplative terms, Richard of St Victor reads the sleep of the disciples in another way: 'The fainting of the three disciples represents the failure of sense, memory and reason in this highest contemplation...in the experience of contemplative ecstasy.' The challenge of contemplation is of continual beholding, watching and waiting, alert and expectant: 'I sleep, yet my heart wakes.'

Gethsemane locates sleep and vigilance at the heart of the passion of Jesus on the night that he was betrayed. The betrayal was not solely the handing over of Jesus by Judas, but was the sin of omission of the disciples in their failure, despite repeated instruction, to be awake and alert. This is the injunction – 'stay awake' – of the parables. As James Alison notes:

> ...the last [parable] before the unfolding of the Passion, refers exactly to the events of the Passion which are to unfold. The coming of the master will take place in the handing over of Jesus, for it is at evening that he hands himself over to the disciples in the form of the Eucharist, at midnight that he is handed over by Judas, who comes when the disciples are asleep...[19]

There is a deep tension and contrast at the heart of the liturgical vigil of Maundy Thursday, with its roots in Gethsemane. The tension is highlighted by the wakefulness of Jesus and the sleep of the disciples. Jesus is awake, watchful, vigilant and attentive to the will of the Father. The disciples are overtaken by sleep (Matthew 26.36–46 and parallels).

There is both a practical and spiritual dimension to the watching the disciples are asked to undertake. First, they have been asked to stay awake to be lookouts for the impending arrival of Judas and the temple police. Second, they have been asked to associate themselves with Jesus' mission in the waking state. Indeed, in Matthew's Gospel they are asked to 'stay awake with me', an intensely personal plea

---

19   Alison, J. (1997) *Living in the End Times: The last things re-imagined.* London: SPCK. p. 148.

(Matthew 26.38b). This is staying awake, and avoiding sleep, as an act of personal commitment and attentiveness to Jesus. Mark does not emphasise that personal association but rather associates sleep with the weakness of the flesh (14.38). Luke is most generous to the sleeping disciples in suggesting that their sleep was 'because of grief' (22.45). Nevertheless, Luke still has the pointed and direct rhetorical question of Jesus: 'Why are you sleeping?' (22.46). Matthew portrays a scene of soporific disciples – 'for their eyes were heavy' and accuses them of 'taking their rest' (26.43). This scene is powerfully captured by Andrea Mantegna (1431–1506) in his painting *The Agony in the Garden* (c.1465). The scene of the sleeping disciples in the garden is not portrayed as an example of God giving sleep to his beloved; rather their submission to sleep represents a failure of theirs to 'stay awake' and be watchful.

Nancy's words are pertinent in relation to this:

> …whoever does not know how not to wake up, whoever remains on the lookout in the hollow of sleep, he, she, is stuck with his or her fear. He is afraid of letting go even of his troubles and cares… But what he fears above all else is not that the difficulties or dangers that these thoughts display threaten to arise as so many failures and defeats on the following day, what he really fears more than these fears themselves is leaving them far behind him and entering the night.[20]

Waking and trusting

Contrasting sleep and prayer, Hauerwas sees the disciples' failure as less about sleep but that the disciples do not pray. By sleeping, the disciples fail to pray and also do not understand the danger at hand but, furthermore, 'retreat into the dreams and fantasies that always tempt us as modes of escape from the reality of Jesus's agony'. While the disciples slept, Jesus could have walked away – he could have walked up the Mount of Olives, through Bethany and away. Rather than that, he kept returning to them because he stared into the darkness and knew he had to bring them through it. Jesus resists sleep as a mode of escape. The second time he comes to the disciples

---

20 Nancy, J-L. *The Fall of Sleep* (2009), trans. C. Mandell. New York: Fordham University Press, p.48.

he does not interrupt their sleep, but he continues to pray. Hauerwas sees in Jesus' prayer the making of his vulnerability to God, in which prayer is an alternative to sleep. Now he knows his hour has come and summons the disciples with the inclusive words 'let us be going'. The disciples' sleeping and Jesus' wakefulness have not driven him to abandon them. So, in contrast to the disciples, Jesus stayed intentionally awake in Gethsemane, and his wakefulness was to enable him to pray. Ben Quash notes that, 'in the Garden of Gethsemane, it was precisely he [Jesus] who stayed awake while others slept – staring into the darkness and wrestling with what it seemed he must do to keep the world afloat'. He continues:

> [Jesus] stayed awake in order to look open-eyed into the face of the world's fallenness, and to find there a task that only he, the obedient one, could perform – and would perform on human beings' behalf. He stayed awake, then, in a way that only he could, accommodating his disciples' inability to stay awake with him.[21]

What Jesus' wakefulness 'achieves', in obedience to the Father, is to make 'it possible – in principle – for them to sleep trustfully again'.

---

21   Quash, B. (2012) *Abiding*. London: Bloomsbury Publishing, p.210.

4

AS THE NIGHT WATCH LOOKS FOR THE MORNING

Sleep is not death, but it is *a* death. In sleep we die to the day that is past, we die to our own ego, and we let go the control of our cares and concerns, which might revisit us through dreams. When we sleep we experience the 'inrush of timelessness' evocative of death.

Yet morning comes, and with it the possibilities of the new day. A Hebrew benediction for the morning goes even further, saying, 'Blessed art Thou, O Lord our God, King of the universe, who creates Thy world every morning afresh.' The act of waking to the new morning puts us in touch with the creative power of God and his life. Kallistos Ware suggests that 'each morning we awake, we are as it were newly created'. The morning hymn of John Keble, intended to be sung on waking, conveys the same message:

> New every morning is the love
> Our wakening and uprising prove;
> Through sleep and darkness safely brought,
> Restored to life, and power, and thought.

'And there was evening and there was morning': sleep configures creatures to the rhythms of the creation and gives confidence to awake to a new creation each day.

This chapter turns our attention to waking. If the notion of *theosomnia* is a robust one, then it must be able to give an account of the act of waking as much as the act of sleeping. A sleep from which one does not wake is death. This is not simply because waking is the absence of sleep, or vice versa. Rather, the relationship between waking and sleeping is one that Christian theology has used from early days, and has direct roots both in the Gospel and in Pauline material. The Psalms also connect waking with new life. The way in which waking from sleep might be understood theologically is through eschatology, the nature of time and resurrection as the ultimate awakening.

The relationship between sleep and death, waking and resurrection is open to much misunderstanding. It also has the capacity for pastoral damage. If sleep is seen as a euphemism for death, then sleep is part of a human avoidance strategy for talking about death directly. This is not tenable in Christian theology. If sleep is used as a metaphor for death, then it becomes a particularly generative metaphor to be embraced and not spurned. In John's Gospel we see the prior problem when sleep is assumed to be used euphemistically rather than literally or metaphorically. This is precisely what the disciples do at the beginning of the account of the death of Lazarus:

> After saying this, Jesus told them, 'Our friend Lazarus has fallen asleep, but I am going there to awaken him.' The disciples said to him, 'Lord, if he has fallen asleep, he will be all right.' Jesus, however, had been speaking about his death, but they thought that he was referring merely to sleep. Then Jesus told them plainly, 'Lazarus is dead. For your sake I am glad I was not there, so that you may believe. But let us go to him.' (John 11.11–15)

There is a further confusion in the account of the raising of Jairus' daughter, which prompts scorn from the onlookers as Jesus says 'she is not dead but sleeping' (Matthew 9.24).

The story of sleep, eschatology and resurrection is rooted in the generative metaphor of sleep for death and waking for resurrection. Eschatology connects sleep and time and how it is time to awake from sleep.

Death, mortality and waking

In Chapter 1 we reflected on mortality in relation to the fall of sleep in the context of the Office of Compline mapping out our preparations to fall asleep, which itself mimics the preparation for death. That drew our attention to the close interplay between the bed laid out for sleep and the deathbed. The story continues as we consider awakening. The deathbed signals the finality of death, but the word cemetery, where the dead lie, points to an awakening, because cemetery means a 'sleeping place' (from the Greek κοιμητήριον).

The grave is rarely conceived as 'a sign of hope that promises resurrection' but rather, as Nancy sees it, as having no other purpose 'than to offer the assurance of a stone or leaden sleep, a sleep of earth or ash, a sleep without sleep and without insomnia, without awakening and without intention, a limitless sleep'. This acknowledges that all will pass away and fall (*tombé*), but does not resonate with the sleep proclaimed in Christian anthropology. Martin Israel, an Anglican priest and doctor, writes that 'all the affairs of the world pass away as we quit the realm of mortal strife in sleep, and later on the death that is the door to a new existence'. This he roots in the primacy of love. In a meditation before sleep he urges:

> Let us therefore flow out in love to all creatures, and especially to our human adversaries, as we prepare to end this day in blessed sleep. The love will proceed even when we are asleep, as it will surely do when we 'quit this mortal frame', as Alexander Pope puts it ('The Dying Christian to his Soul').[1]

Israel speaks of the release that death will bring, along with the underlying ethical imperative of renunciation of possessions and self that is a feature of being mortal:

> The person with the burden of many possessions has greater difficulty in letting them go, as we all shall when we know that greatest sleep which we call death. I am confident that then also we shall awake even more refreshed than during earthly life to share in God's heavenly banquet, before we are sent on to do the work ahead of us, which is to bring the day of God's glory closer to our world, and through it to the entire universe.[2]

Eschatology

During sleep the mortal body is transformed. It is a transformation generated by, or reflected in, different measurable and observable aspects of the body: brain activity; chemical changes, such as rising melatonin levels; posture; and awareness of surroundings. The language of transformation is theologically familiar and it connects us with eschatology.

---

1   Israel, M. (1990) *Night Thoughts*. London: SPCK, p.61.
2   Israel, *Night Thoughts*, p.111.

Sleeping and waking convey eschatological meaning. Baillie gives a treatment of the Psalm text 'As for me I shall see your face in righteousness; when I awake and behold your likeness, I shall be satisfied' (Psalm 17.16). The possible meanings that he considers range from practical to eschatological interpretation. It could mean: 'awaking from a fit of depression to a juster estimate of values'; or, more prosaically, the sheer delight of waking to a new day and its possibilities; or, finally, the eschatological promise of 'the great awakening of resurrection morning'. Equally the Psalm text 'I will lie down and sleep' (Psalm 4.8) could refer to the laying down of existential burdens, or simply the fact of closing the past day, or the act of dying.

This could be profoundly hopeless, as in Jean-Luc Nancy's statement:

> Sleep is not a metamorphosis. At the very most it could be understood as an endomorphosis, as the internal formation or the formation of an interiority where the interior, sealed, seemed wholly projected into the intentions and extensions of wakeful existence. Internal formation, but without a transformation of being.[3]

A theological understanding of sleep in relation to eschatology is that it is profoundly transformative, and therefore hope-filled.

There is another dimension to the transformation of the person: death. Christian anthropology sees life as 'changed, not taken away'. This transformation is much harder to account for because inevitably it is not something that can be measured but only spoken of and represented as an invitation to a mystery beyond present embodied conscious experience. Nevertheless, theology claims to be able to comment on this because of the way in which the resurrection of Jesus decisively opens up what is beyond death, as reflected in biblical revelation. This that sketches out a vision of a transformed and renewed creation to which sleeping and waking are pointers.

---

3   Nancy, J-L. *The Fall of Sleep*, (2009) trans. C. Mandell. New York: Fordham University Press, p.4.

Transformation and time

It is not only transformation of body that is encountered in sleep but also perception of time. Theology speaks of time in two different ways using two Greek words: *chronos* and *kairos*. *Chronos* refers to chronological, measurable time, the division of time and experience into years, days, hours, minutes and so on. The God of Israel, witnessed to in the Bible, works in and through time and history. The Incarnation binds Jesus, so to speak, to chronological time. The language of *chronos* allows the language of promise and the life of the world to come, a time that will come in chronological terms, but when it comes cannot be measured as such. Sirach puts it more directly in the context of mortality: 'Whether life lasts for ten years or a hundred or a thousand, there are no questions asked in Hades' (Sirach 41.4b). This time is known as *kairos,* as is better understood as unmeasured or immeasurable time. This is time for being fulfilled in the moment; it is experiential, qualitative time.

The monastic Hours hallow and mark this time. David Steindl-Rast notes that the term 'Hour' from the Greek *hora*, in the monastic sense, is not to be confused with a segment of 60 minutes of time. It is, 'more a presence than a measurement'. Sleep deals in both. There is a measurable chronological dimension, although the sleeper is unaware of it, alongside the sense of fulfilled time. This fulfilled time through presence is the more generative concept as far as sleep is concerned. Yet, even that is elusive, because clearly the sleeper cannot articulate 'quality' in relation to time whilst asleep. In philosophy, Bergson, of the Vitalist school of thought, made a similar distinction in relation to time, putting an emphasis on *durée*, denoting 'real' or 'lived' time rather than the abstraction of 'clock' time, which continues remote from human experience. McGilchrist traces different understandings of time to the two hemispheres of the brain, noting: 'Time is the context that gives meaning to everything in this world, and conversely everything has meaning for us in this world, everything that has a place in our lives, exists in time.' He suggests that this is not true of abstractions but that 'all that *is* is subject to time'. The sense of passing time is associated with sustained attention, he argues, in the right hemisphere, principally the right prefrontal and parietal cortex, as does the ability to compare duration in time.

Sleep takes human experience to the fringes of the 'eternal sleep' of death; death's proximity to sleep is in the *kairos* sense but not the chronological. This is captured in the Psalms: 'For a thousand years in thy sight are but as yesterday: seeing that is past as a watch in the night. As soon as thou scatterest them they are even as a sleep: and fade away suddenly like grass' (Psalm 90.4, 5).[4] St Paul echoes this: 'we will not all die (Greek *fall asleep*), but we will all be changed, in a moment, in the twinkling of an eye' (1 Corinthians 15.51, 52). Falling asleep as a metaphor for death functions in a number of ways and, in relation to mortality, transformation and time, it becomes a vehicle of a way of speaking about eschatological matters. As a metaphor for death, sleep is not inexhaustible, but language cannot get closer. When related to both *chronos* and *kairos,* sleep does not exist outside time, and yet that is something that may be said of death.

You know what time it is

It would be wrong to infer from the above a thoroughly unambiguous theological relationship between sleep and time. Whilst it is possible to deploy scripture to illustrate the virtues of sleep, it is also possible to argue the other way. Paul's treatment of sleep is highly influential in the Christian tradition's ambivalent attitude towards sleep. Paul's appeal is to wake up, to be alert. Nevertheless, this is not the eradication of sleep but the consciousness of the inverse of falling asleep, and that is the rising from sleep. The Greek word *egēiro* appears not infrequently in the New Testament and can be translated variously as awake, rouse, draw up (as in drawing water) and rise. This is evident in the letter to the Christians of Rome:

> Besides this, you know what time it is, how it is now the moment for you to wake from sleep. For salvation is nearer to us now than when we became believers; the night is far gone, the day is near. Let us then lay aside the works of darkness and put on the armour of light; let us live honourably as in the day, not in revelling and drunkenness, not in debauchery and licentiousness, not in quarrelling

---

4   The NRSV version replaces the word 'sleep' with 'dream'. Either is a legitimate translation; see Anderson, A.A. (1972) *The Book of Psalms: Volume 2.* Grand Rapids, MI: Eerdmans, p.651.

and jealousy. Instead, put on the Lord Jesus Christ, and make no provision for the flesh, to gratify its desires. (Romans 13.11–14)

In this passage Paul deploys sleep as a metaphor for the time of inattentiveness that characterises the darkness of the night – and he contrasts it with the day. The night is the time when people revel in drunkenness, debauchery and licentiousness, and, as it were, have to sleep it off. The people of the day and of the light, disciples, are not caught up in that sort of sleep. They have awoken, been raised up, from a *reasonable and knowing sleep*, since they 'know what time it is' and reject the way of the night and darkness wrapped up in the metaphor of sleep.

In his book *The Epistle to the Romans* Karl Barth teases out the 'knowing of the time' of Romans 13.11, saying that '[b]etween the past and the future – between the times – there is a Moment that is no moment in time'. For Barth this is the moment in which we become present. We face both ways: 'This "Moment" is the eternal Moment – the *Now* – when the past and the future stand still, when the former ceases its going and the latter its coming.' Sleep plays with our concepts of time. We do not live simply by the ordered life of *chronos* but the moments of *kairos*, the sense of fulfilled and fulfilling time: we may seek our eight hours, or an optimum time, of sleep, but knowing that a ten-minute catnap might *feel* as refreshing. Barth's emphasis is that Paul's call in Romans is to live in a life bound in love because 'he who loves is touched by the freedom of God'. This is the mark of children of the day because freedom is found in the Moment. So then, '*Salvation – the day*, the Kingdom of God – being the fulfilment of all time is incomparable.' Barth acknowledges, however, that we do not live outside 'the flux of time' but within it (the Incarnation places Jesus Christ in the flux of time). Indeed, 'for us, too, there must be within this knowledge a place, a time, an occasion for love'.

This is how sleep has an eternal quality to it. Barth's rich exploration of time and moments connects to the moment of waking from sleep. It is an indefinable moment. I can only define it against the condition I am in. I can only say when awake, 'I am not asleep.' As Barth continues, 'the knowledge of the "Moment" must occur in a moment: the turning back to eternity must occur in a time'. Barth speaks of 'an unqualified time of *sleep*'. During this sleeping state humanity is in need of reminding of revelation, recalled to a necessary knowledge and recalled to the freedom of God. Barth goes on to state:

> In so far as this recollection has *not yet* taken place – and when indeed has it ever 'already' taken place? – men are asleep, even the apostle, even the saints, even the lover. Men are sold under time, its property. They lie like pebbles in the 'stream of time', and backwards and forwards the ripples hurry over them.[5]

It is a characteristic of this current time, as ever, that people are incapable of doing what they ought to do and not doing what they ought not to do. There is an ethical void in this soporific time and state because of the distinctions of time and the 'Moment' of eternity. So Barth says, 'There are times that are *near*, and times that are far; there is night-time and there is the time when the day begins to dawn; there are times of sleeping and there are times of awakening.' The absence of ethical living is human failure to wake to the imperative of love and the divine gift already in front of us, so he continues:

> What delays [the Moment's] coming is not the Parousia, but our awakening. Did we but awake…then, neither shall we join the sentimentalists in expecting some magnificent or terrible FINALE, not should we comfort ourselves for its failure to appear by embracing the confident frivolity of modern protestant cultured piety.[6]

Barth's treatment of Romans 13.11 gives a clear and powerful exposition of the Pauline sense of waking from sleep, pivoting on the notion of the moment in which sleep gives way to wakefulness. In contrast to Barth, John Ziesler is rather more prosaic, saying that Paul's phrase 'to wake from sleep' is 'in effect to be watchful, vigilant, ready for the End when it comes'. By invoking Barth we have sought to say that sleep is freighted with even more meaning than Ziesler's reductionist account.

---

5   Barth, K. (1933) *The Epistle to the Romans*, trans. E.C. Hoskyns. Oxford: Oxford University Press, p.499.

6   Barth, *Romans*, p.501.

Sleep and eschatology: timelessness and hope

One of the key theological suppositions in any treatment of time is, as stated above, that God is creator of but not bound by time or any finite action. Rowan Williams describes God's acts as 'undetermined by ours,' which is safeguarded by

> the traditional theological commitments to the timelessness of God, or at least God's non-participation in the same scheme of temporality as ours, and the doctrine of creation from nothing are very far from being abstract and speculative matters for the believer.[7]

Understood in this way God prompts 'a change in how we understand our being-in-time'; Williams continues: 'God's difference from our temporality leaves us with a time that can be seen as *given*, as an opportunity for growth or healing, since no disaster is finally and decisively destructive.' Whilst Christian hope is always to be read in that light, it does not guarantee happy endings since. Drawing on this hope, Jean Pierre de Caussade notes that this would trivialise the doctrine of divine providence. Such hope 'is an assurance that time is always there for restoration; that we are never rendered incapable of action and passion, creating and being created, by any event'. In *Church Dogmatics* Karl Barth sets his reflections on sleep within the Doctrine of Creation, in a section on 'Ending Time'. This locates sleep within the created order and in relation to the creator. From this a connection can be made with the doctrine of grace which speaks of the giftedness of creation and what God bestows upon his creatures, thus meeting their needs.

Sleep is a phenomenon in which 'God's difference from our temporality is seen': God neither slumbers nor sleeps. Sleep gives a renewed perspective on being-in-time in which hope is accounted for in a time of restorative grace from which the person awakens. De Caussade puts it in this way:

> Lord, may I not likewise say that thou holdest asleep on thy bosom all thy children during the night of faith, that thou takest pleasure in causing an infinite number of infinitely various sentiments to pass through their souls, sentiments which *au fond* are but holy and

---

7   Williams, R. (2000) 'Interiority and Epiphany.' In *On Christian Theology*. Oxford: Blackwell, p.249.

mysterious dreamings? In the state in which the night and their sleep places them, they experience authentic and painful terrors, anguish and worries which thou wilt dissipate and transform on the day of glory into true and solid joys.[8]

The transformation of which de Caussade speaks has a transformative dimension rendered in time. The transformative, and eschatological, character of sleep is connected to another 'moment' that is impossible to identify, that of the resurrection. No moment of resurrection has ever been identified, and indeed the impulse to do that has been resisted: the 'moment' is given three days in which to happen. It is, though, at the moment of the death of Jesus, when the curtain of the temple is torn in two, that Matthew relates that 'the tombs were opened, and many bodies of the saints who had fallen asleep were raised (*egēiro*)' (Matthew 27.52). Like the story of Lazarus, this raises questions about identity and the character of risen life before the general resurrection and, if seen in diachronic terms, the nature of time itself. Again, the metaphor of sleep is deployed so as to open up the ways of reading such accounts.

Eschatology and the inhabitability of time

Eschatology is the wondering about human destiny and the 'last things' that are beyond sight and comprehension, yet witnessed to in scripture. It is not that eschatology is only ever about what goes on after death or matters affecting the 'life of the world to come'; rather that it takes hold of life and living it abundantly in the light of what is known of what is to come. This is something of the re-imagining of the last things that James Alison invites reflection on. Alison describes the 'Time of Abel' in which the young Abel returns, and in doing so Cain can be forgiven through Abel's 'insistent presence which gives Cain time to recover his story, and [over time]…begin to construct another story'. 'This is the story,' Alison says, 'of which we speak when we speak of the human story in its working out starting from the resurrection.' In constructing his argument for the Time of Abel, as the generative space in which a story of forgiveness is woven

---

8   Caussade, J-P. (1933) *Self-Abandonment to Divine Providence*. Ed. P.H. Rannière, trans. A. Thorold. london: Burns, Oates and Washbourne, p.122.

into human lives, Alison uses sleep as an image. This deployment of sleep both captures its eschatological dimension and the parables of the kingdom and of the end times that Jesus employs:

> Let us imagine [Cain] in a hut...trying to sleep. Sleep does not come to him easily, because he has a presage of danger, and at times he stays half awake through the night. This night is no different, but suddenly he is fully awake when he realizes that someone has entered, burrowing a small hole in the wall. Cain is frightened: it will be either a thief or a murderer.[9]

Alison's 'parable' goes on to imagine the brothers' reconciliation, saying that 'the process of remembering his brother is not at all pleasant for [Cain], since at every awakening to what had really happened, it shakes him to see what has been driving him since then'. It is more than simply that the language of sleep is used, but rather the awareness of the self as a being-in-time that Alison is using and is significant.

Sleep is a theological tool that lends itself to eschatology and transformation, including the transformation of restoration and re-conciliation. The redemption of memory is part of the way in which time enables transformation. Much of this is about being in the world as much as being in time, in the sense that the way in which persons are aware of what they are and who they become is spatially bound. Sleep subverts that awareness because it both binds, to a fixed place, and frees, because the very act of being asleep unbinds the sleeper from the tangibility of relationships which may be life giving or destructive.

The way that a person is a being-in-time and being-in-the-world has thrown up eschatological questions throughout the history of the Church: flight from the world or immersion in it has been a tension within Christianity from the very beginning. This is reflected in early monasticism, iconoclasm, enculturation and ethical and moral debates. Sometimes the 'flight' from the world is a total renunciation of it, and sometimes in a sense of service back to the world by withdrawing from it. There are parallels with sleep as a state of the

---

9   Alison, J. (1997) *Living in the End Times: The Last Things Re-Imagined.* London: SPCK, p.133.

body, since the body is visibly different, transformed, from waking to sleeping. It is a flight from the waking life, and *conscious* engagement in relationships in the world. It is also a withdrawal that enables the sleeper to 'return' to the waking life renewed and potentially with more to offer.

The ability to inhabit the world is picked up in Christian discourse around the nature of the human body. Some traditions so revile the works of the flesh that they associate the body with that corruption; both ancient and contemporary forms of Gnosticism show that. This has an eschatological bearing on the understanding of human destiny and the last things. Should the desire of the Christian be to remain in the world and continue to serve within it? This is the challenge of dualism, which is essentially the splitting of soul from body. Sarah Coakley asks if the 'post-modern *intellectual* obsessions with "body"' are another 'evasive ploy' that fuels and feeds off 'manifestations of death-denial'. However, rather than that, Coakley explores the possibility of seeing the body theologically as 'longing for transformation into the divine'. That collapses dualism and binary polarity. Dualism challenges embodiment and thus how sleep might be understood. Indeed, it takes sleep as an eschatological concept beyond that which it can bear metaphorically.

Soul sleep

The foregoing survey of time and brief reflection on eschatology opens up the contentious area of 'soul sleep'. In terms of what happens when we die, Stephen T. Davis rejects the idea of temporary nonexistence as 'by a wide margin the minority report, so to speak, of Christian theology'. It is misleadingly called 'soul sleep'. Davis gives two clear reasons why the association with sleep is inappropriate. First, because the soul does not sleep during the interim period – it does not exist – and, second, because 'sleeping is essentially a bodily activity, and during the interim period the body is incapable of any activity'. For Luther, 'Scripture applies the term "sleep" to those who are placed into the coffin and grave. These people, however,... will simply be transformed or changed.' This is what leads to the Anabaptist adoption of the 'soul sleep' position which believes there is 'an intermediate *state*, but not an intermediate *place*'. This state is seen as being analogous to human sleep in which the soul continues, but does not exist consciously.

'Soul sleep' is a doctrine searching for texts to justify it. It is something Martin Luther came to slowly, as Jürgen Moltmann suggests, 'after a little wavering'. In it he 'imagined the state of the dead as a sleep, in which the person remains so deeply asleep that this state is dreamless, unconscious, without any feeling, and even "removed from space and time"'. This reading draws from Paul's assertion that Christ is 'the first fruits of those who have fallen asleep' (1 Corinthians 15.20), which, Luther suggests, means that 'this remnant of death is to be regarded as no more than a deep sleep, and that the future resurrection of our body will not differ from suddenly awaking from such a deep sleep'. Joseph Ratzinger commends Luther in this for 'at least [getting] to grips with the issue by representing man between death and resurrection as "asleep"'. This raises questions about how physical sleep is really to be understood eschatologically and, within that, what the nature place of dreams and nature of consciousness is. Luther's image connects the body to sleep but is flawed because sleep is not an unconscious time, in the sense of the brain not working, that dreams are integral to sleeping and that bodies, whilst feeling a certain timelessness, still exist in time. Importantly however Luther does envisage this state as involving his whole body, not a dualist separation.

This question for Luther, and others, arises because of the eschatological question about the human destiny at the moment of death. As Thiselton asks, will there be 'an immediate departure to be with Christ or an intermediate state before the Resurrection?' He sees both possibilities as thoroughly biblical: the yearning to depart to something that has already happened (Philippians 1.23; 2 Corinthians 5.6), and the awareness of going to a 'place' where all are yet to be raised (1 Corinthians 15.52). Whilst both are scripturally valid and neither can be said to take precedence over the other, they are not mutually exclusive. Drawing on Moltmann's work, Thiselton suggests that one way of reconciling 'the immediate departure' approach and the 'intermediate state' approach might be to say 'that a state of waiting is still "in Christ"'. Moltmann's summary is compelling because it is so humane:

Christians know that they are safely hidden in Christ (Col. 3.3),… but they are not yet in the new world of the future… The dead are dead, and are not yet risen, but they are already 'in Christ' and are with him in the way to the future… Neither death nor life…will be able to separate us from the love of God that is in Christ Jesus (Rom. 8.38–39).[10]

For Thiselton this goes much of the way, but not quite the whole way, to explaining the tension. He uses Gilbert Ryle's 'paradox' of the participant and the logician to explore it further. The illustration Thiselton uses is a 'homely analogy' which compares what might be said to children as they try to sleep on the night of Christmas Eve:

We might say, 'The sooner you fall asleep, the sooner Christmas morning will be here.' As *participants* who are deeply involved, they will find this true. But as *'observers'* parents or other adults will find *plenty to do while the children sleep*: there may be presents to wrap and label; for some, midnight Communion to attend; and so on. They will meet early on Christmas morning; but for the children the experience will be immediate. However 'sleeping' is only part of a randomly chosen analogy. It is simply a convenient example which shows how different the 'participant' and 'observer' perspective may be.[11]

Thiselton at once exposes the inadequacy of sleep as an analogy for the last times, qua Luther, but also its instinctive helpfulness in that it holds the tension between time and timelessness and between consciousness and unconsciousness. He also shows that the one who sleeps and the one who beholds the sleep experience time and place differently: the *observer* and *participant* experience the act of falling asleep, or dying, in radically different ways.

'Soul sleep' also does not honour the way in which Paul uses 'sleep' and the rabbinic and biblical *milieu* of his thinking. Indeed Joseph Ratzinger is more emphatic: 'the idea of a sleep of death, in the sense of an unconscious state spanning the period between death and the end of the world, is an unfounded piece of archaizing which

---

10 Moltmann, J. (1996) *The Coming of God: Christian Eschatology*. London: SCM Press, p.105.

11 Thiselton, A.C. (2012) *The Last Things: A New Approach*. London: SPCK, pp.73–74.

no New Testament text warrants'. Equally, as Ratzinger notes, there have been two phases in Paul's understanding of the coming *parousia*: first that he would experience it personally, and a second phase in which the immediacy diminished. Ratzinger detects that evolution but also draws attention to the way in which the image of sleep occurs in Paul's eschatological thought. For Ratzinger the work of Hoffman is important in analysing the semantic field of the language of sleep. In summary, sleep was a euphemism for dying, and for being dead, both in the Hebrew and Hellenistic spheres. It comprised 'the idea of unconsciousness, as well as the more positive notion of the peace enjoyed by the just as distinct from sinners'. Hoffman demonstrates to Ratzinger's satisfaction that '[Paul's] use of [sleep] is uncommitted' and that, accordingly, 'no inferences can be drawn about his views of the condition of the dead'. Paul gives 'Christological heart and depth' to his Pharisaic and Rabbinic teaching that means that 'those who have died in Christ are alive: this is the fundamental certitude which was able to exploit contemporary Jewish conceptions for its own purpose'.

Time and transformation are two key features of the Christian eschatological imagination. And, as has been shown, both are features of sleep. Sleep feeds and informs Christian eschatological vocabulary but has its dangers too. Moltmann sees sleep as a form of inactivity, whereas 'resting in the freedom of God' is not, 'but it is also no state of fulfilment like that imagined in eternal blessedness'. Rather than sleep, 'the dead "watch" and "wait" for their perfection and "experience" their healing and transfiguration into the image of God'. Sleep precludes vigilance; but the way sleep is understood theologically means it provides the perfect foil for understanding what vigilance is and what the believer who intentionally breaks sleep looks for.

Resurrection bodies

In the Bible sleep is used as a euphemism for death, and as such it is applied to the language regarding human destiny beyond death. The resurrection of Jesus Christ changes that. In 1 Corinthians 15, Paul applies sleep in two ways: first, to refer to those who have already died (vv.6 and 18) and, second, to Christ as the 'first fruits' of those who have died (v.20). The *New Revised Standard Version* of the Bible wants to remove the euphemism by translating the word for 'fallen asleep' to 'died'. Yet removing the ambiguity that the euphemism leaves open also robs the word of its richness and the metaphorical freight it can bear, which is significant. It is also the case that when Paul wishes to use the word 'dead' he does so (1 Thessalonians 4.16–17; 1 Corinthians 15.22–23).

Hebrew thought

N.T. Wright carefully explores ancient pagan and pre-Christian texts to examine them for traces of the concept of resurrection. He says of the Hebrew Scriptures that 'for much of the Old Testament the idea of resurrection is, to put it at its strongest, deeply asleep, only to be woken by echoes from later times and texts'. Wright surveys many sources and, in passing, draws out key themes connecting resurrection and sleep. 'Sheol' is the biblical name for 'the dark, deep regions, [and] the land of forgetfulness', which could be a good description of sleep itself; however, Sheol is also a place 'where the presence of YHWH himself is withdrawn'. The notion of 'sleeping with one's ancestors' is a further Hebrew image that is clearly not literal but often referred to an ancestral burial place, or the fact of death shared with pre-deceased ancestors. Wright suggests that, in this reference to sleep, 'they were not completely non-existent, but to all intents and purposes they were, so to speak, next to nothing'. Death, unlike sleep, was (and is) the end of a mortal life, but Wright suggests that 'the dead might be asleep; they might be almost nothing at all; but hope lived on within the covenant and promise of YHWH'. So even in the sleep of Sheol, or with one's ancestors, God's watchfulness continues.

Wright is clear that Hebrew thought reflected in, for example, the book of Daniel – 'many of those who sleep in the dust of the earth shall awake' (Daniel 12.2a) – shows that the metaphor of 'sleep' for death was already widespread and that sleeping in the dust of the earth 'was a clear way of referring to the dead'. So at the same time it was natural to continue the metaphor by using 'awake' to denote bodily resurrection. However, this was clearly 'not a different sort of sleep, but its abolition'. We shall see this further breakdown in Jesus' use of sleep as a metaphor for death. Thus, for Wright, awakening and resurrection is seen 'not as a *reconstrual* of life after death, but the *reversal* of death'. This has a bearing upon how sleep is thought of as a metaphor for death: 'The language of awakening is not a new, exciting way of talking about sleep. It is a way of saying that a time will come when sleepers will sleep no more. Creation itself, celebrated throughout the Hebrew scriptures, will be reaffirmed, remade.' This gives a foundation from which an exploration of the metaphor of sleep in relation to death can be made and more particularly resurrection in the accounts of the raising of Lazarus and Jairus' daughter. This is the 'Christological heart' of how sleep is seen in the light of the resurrection.

Early Christian thought: 1 Thessalonians

Sleep as a metaphor for death in the New Testament has pastoral as well as doctrinal and biblical interpretation implications. Wright examines Paul's understanding of an 'intermediate state' between bodily death and bodily resurrection with particular reference to 1 Thessalonians. In this Paul deploys the sleep metaphor for those who have died. This enables him 'to speak of people who are currently asleep but who will one day wake up again', which echoes Daniel 12.2. That is to say, sleep provides a metaphor for the conviction that the sleep of death is not the last state for the body. As we have seen, the image can be misused, and Wright colourfully expresses that metaphor taken too literally when he describes those who pick up 'a vivid Pauline metaphor and [run] down the street waving it about'. So, he sees no justification for the metaphor of sleep leading to speculation about 'the sleep of the soul' as 'a time of unconscious post-mortem existence prior to the reawakening of resurrection'. The metaphor can only be pushed as far as saying that 'it is the body that "sleeps" between death and resurrection'. In all probability, Wright suggests, 'Paul is using the language of sleeping and waking simply as a way of contrasting a stage of temporary inactivity, not necessarily unconsciousness, with a subsequent one of renewed activity.' This is further illustrated by the language of those who have fallen asleep still living with the Lord (5.10), being 'with Jesus' (4.14) or 'with the Lord' (4.17). This is where sleep is an inadequate metaphor for death and resurrection since, as Wright notes, there is a 'tension inherent in belonging to the risen Messiah on the one hand and being bodily dead, and yet not raised, on the other'.

As Chapter 2 showed, sleep can be a metaphor for inattentiveness, and wakefulness is the state of being alert to God. In terms of exploring sleep and resurrection, waking is not just about being alert and staying awake, but waking early so that when the day dawns those who are already up and awake will not be startled by it. Christians, Paul says, are 'children of the light, of the day' (1 Thessalonians 5.4–8). The ethical implication of this is that Christians should be, in the here and now, living out in their conduct the ways of the day of the Lord. Being awake is to be resurrection people, because whilst our bodies still need to be transformed we are, in terms of resurrection-related imagery, already 'awake', and must stay that way. Sleeping and waking are primarily resurrection imagery, and through this imagery Paul offers an *inaugurated eschatology* which draws on the night and day imagery of Genesis.

Christians are already, in that sense, awake. Baptism awakens us to that new reality: a splash of cold water awakens us to resurrection living. The letter to the Ephesians contains a wakeup call: 'Sleeper, awake! Rise from the dead, and Christ will shine on you' (Ephesians 5.14). Wright suggests that this quotation is from an early Christian song or poem. If that is the case then sleep imagery has been embedded in Christian thought from the very beginning. Sleeping, waking and rising from the dead are intimately connected, and sleep, as a metaphor, itself becomes exhausted. This is the rising to the new and glorious day of each day of creation and 'the day which the Lord hath made, we will rejoice and be glad in it' (Psalm 118.24).

Sleep through resurrection eyes: the death of a euphemism

Thiselton explores 1 Corinthians 15 with the Pauline construal of the 'Christological heart' as the key to unlocking the Christian language of resurrection, which is being *in Christ*. So, he notes:

> The metaphor of **sleep** for death on the part of believers who are 'in Christ' was important in the earliest Christian faith, for the logical 'grammar' of **sleep** (koimao) carries with it the expectation of *awaking to a new dawn and a new day*, ie the expectation of resurrection and the gift of renewed life and vigor [sic] (cf. v. 51). It also anticipates the triumphant hope of the removal of *the sting*

(to kentron, v. 55) of death when God through Christ has dealt with sin (v. 56).[12]

This 'grammar of sleep' is important. Typically the problem with using sleep as a euphemism for death is that it cheapens what death is about and denies its finality. And yet this is what the resurrection of Jesus Christ does: death is conquered and loses its sting. Thiselton cites Oscar Cullmann and Wolfhart Pannenberg who have explored this 'profound image':

> Cullmann compares the 'wrongness' of death in pre-Christian biblical tradition with the deceptive optimism concerning death as 'release' from the body in such Greek thinkers as Socrates. Only after the horror of Christ's death can death 'lose its sting'. Hence while 'with sublime calm Socrates drinks the hemlock...Jesus...cries, "My God, my God, why hast Thou forsaken me?"' (Mark 15.37)... This is not 'death as a friend'. This is death in all its frightful horror... *the last enemy* of God (Cullmann's italics). Because it is God's enemy it separates us from God. But once a person has grasped 'the horror of death' it becomes possible to join Paul in the hymn of victory: 'Death is swallowed up – in victory' (1 Corinthians 15.54–55). Hence, if a Christian encounters death as an experience which has lost its sting, 'the most usual image for Paul is: 'they are asleep'... Death has lost its horror. Pannenberg points out that the logic of 'waking' is entailed in the notion of sleep: it promises resurrection: 'The familiar experience of being awakened and rising from sleep serves as a parable for the completely unknown destiny expected for the dead.'[13]

As Thiselton says of the metaphor of sleep, '[it] regularly denotes the experience of death for Christians as pregnant with hope and becomes a standard term'.

It is out of resurrection that the eschatological dimension of sleep is illustrated in this language of the early Christians, specifically Paul's view of eschatological imminence. This turns on the phrase

---

12 Thiselton, A.C. (2000) *The First Epistle to the Corinthians*. Grand Rapids, MI: William B. Eerdmans, p.1220.

13 Thiselton, *The First Epistle to the Corinthians*, pp.603–604.

in 1 Corinthians 15.51, *pantes hou koimethesometha*. Thiselton highlights its three possible meanings:

> either (i) *none of us shall sleep,* i.e., the Parousia will intervene before any believer dies; or (ii) *not all of us shall* (as some of us shall) *sleep* i.e., the Parousia will come in the lifetime of some of us; or (iii) *not all of us humans shall sleep,* i.e., the Parousia will interrupt human history at some point *sooner or later* (time unspecified).[14]

Sleep as a resurrection metaphor has the capacity to generate this eschatological language. The last trumpet suggests both a signal of proclamation but also a wakeup call. It also connects this eschatological language to the image of the watchman who is deliberately awake whilst others sleep. Christ is the watchman par excellence who slept in the tomb and is raised, and by incorporation into his life shares with the Father, in the power of the Spirit, the capacity to raise all people. It is only if Christ has not been raised from the dead that those who have fallen asleep (or, in the *New Revised Standard Version,* 'died') have truly perished, never to waken. That is the sleep of Sheol.

Dead or sleeping?

We saw above that Jesus' declaration that Lazarus had fallen asleep and needed to be awakened caused confusion amongst the disciples. Paul's treatment of death, sleep and resurrection in 1 Thessalonians and 1 Corinthians 15 informs how we may read John 11 and Luke 8 – Lazarus and the raising of Jairus' daughter – with a Christological heart.

And yet a problem remains. In Wright's work on resurrection, sleep is a recurrent metaphor for death, and waking for resurrection. Wright suggests that, in these two passages, 'The disciples' reaction, taking "sleep" literally, shows that for John at least, as for Mark in the story of Jairus' daughter, this was not so habitual metaphor for death as to leave no room for explanation.' There is ambiguity in the Gospels around sleep and death. This is illustrated in the misunderstandings of the disciples and the mocking of Jairus' family. The problem is illustrated as an issue in biblical translation: how should the words

---

14   Thiselton, *The First Epistle to the Corinthians,* p.1293.

koimao and *katheudo* be translated? They both mean 'to sleep' and are used across the New Testament.

In an apparent effort to de-euphemise the word 'sleep', the *New Revised Standard Version* translates *koimao* as it appears in 1 Corinthians 15 as 'though some *have died*' rather than 'some *have fallen asleep*'. A footnote confirms that the Greek is 'fallen asleep'. This sucks out the meaning from a key metaphor and glosses over the interplay of the narrative in the accounts of Lazarus and Jairus' daughter that leads the hearers and reader to understand that these events are connected to the resurrection of Jesus Christ.

In the case of Jairus' daughter the girl's *sleep* has been another occasion in which God's resurrection power in Jesus has been demonstrated. The reaction to this is scornful because they knew she was dead. As Evans notes, '[h]ere death is not spoken of as sleep but is contrasted with it – "she is not dead but is dead" would be nonsense'. The verbs used in the New Testament for resurrection, *egeirein*, 'to raise up', and *anistanai*, 'to get up', can also both mean 'to awake out of sleep'. The wordplay is used in Ephesians 5 and John 11.11–13. Wright comments:

> The mention of 'sleep' leads the mind naturally to the description of the girl's 'awakening'. Jesus' word of command (Mark and Luke only) is *egeire*, 'arise', which in Mark translates the Aramaic word *talitha koum*. When the girl awakens, the verb used by Mark and Luke is *aneste*, and in Matthew is *egerthe*.[15]

The key point in the use of sleep is that a Christian will 'certainly think of Jesus' own resurrection as a larger and greater instance of the same sort of astonishing power'. Wright notes that no one in the story expects resurrection in the way that a post-resurrection gospel writer or reader knows it: for them Jairus' daughter, as Lazarus, will die again some day; the evangelists 'end up telling a story about Jesus going through death and out the other side'.

The defining text for Barth in his consideration of sleep within his *Church Dogmatics* is from the Raising of Lazarus as Jesus says to Martha, 'I am the resurrection and the life. Those who believe in me, even though they die, will live' (John 11.25). Barth says that in this

---

15   Wright, N.T. (2003) *The Resurrection of the Son of God*. London: SPCK, pp.404–405.

text the New Testament's conviction is that 'the "death" in death can be abolished'. As the story of Lazarus demonstrates, Barth notes, this achievement is not within human control but is 'always the result of God's extraordinary intervention'. Barth sees the final revelation in the coming again of Christ, 'in which the exaltation that has already occurred in Jesus Christ will be made manifest'. This will apply to the dead as much as to the living (citing 1 Thessalonians 4.16f), hence why the language of sleep is so pregnant with meaning since they sleep 'in Christ' (1 Corinthians 15.18) and 'in Jesus' (1 Thessalonians 4.14). 'Even though they die [they] will live': 'Death,' says Barth, 'now wears a guise in which we can look it in the face.'

The King slept

The confident adoption of sleep in relation to death and resurrection and, in an eschatological sense, as a generative metaphor and not as a linguistic masking agent is shown in post-resurrection writing of which two examples will be given.

Luke's account of the death of Stephen (Acts 7.54–end) illustrates this confidence in the sleep metaphor. Stephen dies during a highly traumatic lynching which bears features of the Passion of Christ. Luke Timothy Johnson notes these distinct echoes not least in the phrase 'when he said this, he died', the words used of the death of Jesus on the cross in Luke 23.46. The significant difference is that the word for 'died' (or 'expired', breathe one's last) is replaced with the word for 'falling asleep'. The benignity of falling asleep sits at odds with a violent death. So appropriating sleep as an image of that sort of death is hard. Barth seeks to distinguish *being* asleep from *falling* asleep. This leads him to say that, since Jesus has won the victory, 'all the [New Testament Christians] had to do was to fall asleep'. It is hard to conceive Stephen's death as being one in which all he had to do was fall asleep, and yet, Barth suggests, 'we really look to Jesus Christ, who, as "the first fruits of them that slept"…robbed death of its sting and brought life and immortality to light even when they were *in extremis*, so that this death could not be anything but a falling asleep'.

This is about looking at someone who has 'fallen asleep' and seeing that person as delivered from death even in their dying.

Thus for Barth the early Christians never sought to ask what it is like to be dead or speculating on an intermediate state but rather holding on to the confession 'I am the resurrection and the life', and, he says, 'in the light of this hope they came to see in the visible process of dying the last conclusive symptom of a life surrounded by the peace of God'. So the move from euphemism to metaphor is completed, a metaphor freighted with the biblical witness of those who have already fallen asleep, the proclamation that God gives his beloved rest and watches over his people unceasingly and sealed in the resurrection of Jesus Christ from the dead.

The second example is from an anonymous 'Ancient Paschal Homily' for Holy Saturday. In it Jesus is described as the 'King who sleeps' following his death, and because of this, 'the earth was in terror and was still, because God slept in the flesh and raised up those who were sleeping from the ages. God has died in the flesh, and the underworld has trembled.' The homily imagines how Christ, the New Adam, now in the regions of death, goes to seek out the first Adam: 'And grasping his hand he raises him up, saying: "Awake, O sleeper, and arise from the dead, and Christ shall give you light."' The use of sleep as a resurrection metaphor is striking in the call to awaken and arise: 'Come forth, and those in darkness: Have light, and those who sleep: Rise.'

Even the crucifixion, a traumatic death as in the stoning of Stephen, is seen in the light of the sleep metaphor: 'I slept on the cross and a sword pierced my side, for you, who slept in paradise and brought forth Eve from your side. My side healed the pain of your side; my sleep will release you from your sleep in Hades.' This is vivid and immediate language and reclaims sleep as a metaphor and does not side-line it as pastorally unsafe or damaging.

Depictions of the resurrection of Jesus Christ in art juxtapose the vigorous waking Jesus with sleeping guards in various poses of discomfort around the tomb. The guards are sleeping because they see neither the power of Christ nor the 'capacious metaphor' of sleep. Ratzinger captures what has happened with sleep, that sleep is 'a portmanteau term for being dead – a term which Christians filled with their own content, namely the idea of (conscious) life with the Lord'.

CONCLUSION

Timothy Radcliffe tells the story of a grandfather and his grandson at Mass.[1] At the homily the bishop was preaching interminably. The grandfather dozed off, at which point the bishop, looking accusingly at the grandson, said, 'Wake up the old man', to which the grandson replies, 'You wake him. You made him fall asleep in the first place.'

Sleep can get everywhere, and Radcliffe's story echoes a scene in Acts of the Apostles. On that occasion, it is St Paul himself who is preaching at some length. The young man Eutychus was sitting by a window and clearly the fresh air could not alleviate the onset of sleep. Eutychus sank into a deep sleep and fell from the window and was picked up, apparently dead. The apostle broke off his sermon to declare that there was life in the young man yet. Paul continued to speak until dawn. Acts does not relate if Eutychus made it through the rest of the night or if he retired home. There is a certain playfulness when sleep is referred to in the Church, not least when related to the merits of preachers, even if of apostolic credentials.

There is a deeper story that we have sought to tell in this exploration of theology, and sleep is one of a deepening understanding of God's grace. Our bodies can rest easy, safe in the knowledge that God watches over us in our sleeping vulnerability, that our dreams and fantasies at night need not take hold of us and that we will awaken to a new dawn and all that it suggests in terms of promise and hope. This is captured in the words of a hymn: 'be thou my best thought in the day and the night / both waking and sleeping, thy presence my light'.

This theological account of sleep touches the doctrines of creation, grace and redemption, through examining eschatological thinking and the continued fallout from the resurrection of Jesus Christ. We have seen that the primary place in which this theology has been

---

1   Radcliffe, T. (2012) *Taking the Plunge: Living Baptism and Confirmation*. London: Bloomsbury.

formed is in liturgical practice, notably the Liturgy of the Hours, and in hymnody and traditional prayer practices.

Much of what has been written in this book could have been said in most phases of Christian history. Indeed, we have heard voices from previous Christian centuries, from patristic to early modern eras and from those writing and praying at the time of the Enlightenment. Arguably those voices reflect a time when sleep was feared and, as Roger Ekirch makes clear, there was a vivid and arguably over-imaginative appreciation of the terrors of the night. Henry Nevil Payne (1672–1710) wrote: 'Solitude, the night and fear makes all my danger double to appear.' It would be all too easy to attribute superstition and fear to the Christian approach to sleep. *Theosomnia* does not see sleep as an affliction or state of anxiety in its essence; quite the contrary, it is a time of grace and posture of being oneself without inhibition before God.

The overarching concept we have explored is that of *theosomnia*. It speaks of a loving God who holds us in love at all times, waking and sleeping. It calls us to vigilance and watching but assures of protection and oversight, so that we may sleep easy in our beds. Going further, sleep, as a gift of God, has a sacramental quality. There is an outward and visible sign: shut eyes, obvious posture and such like; there is an inward and spiritual grace, refreshment, renewal and, perhaps, dreams. God's grace is bestowed in the particular context of sleep and, like a sacrament, there can be a good feeling on coming away from it, but equally it is effectual even if the benefit is not perceived.

A theology of sleep is an opportunity to reconsider a fundamental aspect of human existence and Christian discipleship. Sleep dissociates human beings from their own egos, ambitions and the projections of others. It immobilises human wilfulness for a period of time. And yet it is a graced time in which the creature is sustained beyond his or her own conscious capacities. It asks how creatures exist in time and what sustains them. It reconnects people to their creatureliness and being made in God's image and likeness and attunes them to the rhythms of creation. In the mystery of sleep the self is not annihilated; it does not migrate: sleep, seen Christologically, is about *kenosis* and not annihilation.

So where does this exploration take us today? As we conclude I will sketch out some of the areas which I believe this theology of sleep has an impact on. These areas speak to the worshipping life of the Church; inform the lives of disciples today; and provide an apologetic for the language that Christians use in discourse around death, wellbeing and the integrity of the human body and what it means to be human.

Being human in a busy world

Time is not my enemy

'For everything there is a season, and a time for every matter under heaven,' writes Qoheleth, the Preacher in the book of Ecclesiastes (Ecclesiastes 3.1). In a familiar passage he accounts for human behaviour in binary terms: 'a time to be born and to die, to plant and to pluck up what is planted, a time to keep silence and a time to speak' and so on (Ecclesiastes 3.2–8). It is curious then that he omitted the apparently obvious: 'a time to wake and a time to sleep'. It is beyond the scope of this book to speculate on the reasons for that omission, but there are three intriguing reasons why Qoheleth, the Preacher, is worth paying attention to with regard to sleep. First is his sense of the fleeting quality of everything. The breathlessness of the Hebrew word *hebel*, often translated as 'vanity' or 'futility', echoes the breathlessness of sleep, since during sleep breathing patterns change and consciousness and awareness of breathing goes. Second, sleep itself is often seen as a vain, if not thoroughly futile, pursuit. And yet breathing continues. Third, it is *hebel* to try and chase one's breath when one is asleep: even the person who is awake cannot succeed at that. Qoheleth writes about the lot of the person who toils during the day; he notes, 'for all their days are full of pain, and their work is a vexation; even at night their minds do not rest. This also is vanity' (Ecclesiastes 2.23). This has a distinctly contemporary ring to it.

The connection between sleep and time is very relevant to a pastoral consideration of mortality and learning that time is not our enemy. This is less about *kairos*, as we explored in Chapter 3, and more about *chronos*. Sleep highlights human grappling with the fear of vanity, *hebel*, and nothingness. It is trying to capture what James Alison describes when he says:

...it is part of learning that time is not my enemy, but [that time] is very spacious, and I do not need to succeed immediately, or to order, because it is eternal life that is behind the hints of creativity which are being born.[2]

Sleep confronts creatures with mortality and ultimately short-circuits Pelagian notions of salvation. Sleep graces our embodied lives lived in time.

Sleep and indispensability

The helplessness of sleep – helplessness in the sense of the inability to control and dictate – is an antidote to the way in which time can be ungracefully treated. The global culture, sometimes coined '24/7', generated and sustained by global financial markets, rolling news and air travel, has bred with it an attitude towards sleep in which sleep is seen as an inconvenience and a weakness. The phrase 'power nap' was coined to give a macho work culture permission to rest. Sociologists of sleep describe the 24-hour society and its consequences on those who work through the night, shift-workers, and those who travel and suffer jetlag. In their brief introduction to sleep, Lockley and Foster comment that features of contemporary life are 'chipping away at our time for sleep'. They identify the key to all this activity as 'the ability to light the night' which, they suggest, sees a transfer of power: 'the power to remove darkness was once held only by deities, but the ability to light the night fell into mortal hands at the end of the nineteenth century, with the development and widespread installation of electric incandescent lighting'. That is as may be, but still people sleep irrespective of who turns the lights out.

Christian theology has never suggested that the night would be expunged, or sleep eradicated. The issue is not around the ability to light the night but rather the human propensity to use technology to its own ends and often to its own cost. Then we see that the diminution of sleep is a symptom of human inability to face the debilitation of night and the sleep that goes with it. The implication is that time is our enemy. The reality of the 24/7 society changes the balance of

---

2   Alison, J. (2010) *Broken Hearts and New Creations: Intimations of a Great Reversal.* London: Darton, Longman and Todd, p.69.

perception of night and day, waking and sleeping. Sleep is no longer seen as a gift of God or even about natural rhythms of the body; it becomes something that can be 'grabbed' or 'snatched'. As well as being deeply concerning for health, societal attitudes to sleep play to a tendency, as prevalent in the Church as in wider society, that says: to be busy is to be valid; to be asleep is a failure in use of time. A theosomniac reading of sleep sees sleep as a means of hallowing time. The Church has the responsibility to restate that (God given) time is our friend, not our enemy.

Another aspect of the implicit assumption that to be very busy is to be very important is the pursuit of indispensability and its attendant activism. Sleep becomes a casualty of the 24-hour way of life both as a biological good and as a moral and theological imperative. Echoing the storm on the Sea of Galilee, the 24/7, never sleeping society is a storm of busyness. Sleep gets squeezed, with consequences, as researchers tell us, for mental and physical health. What is more, the squeezing of sleep becomes a sign of a dangerous heresy of indispensability. It is as if we are caught up in a frenetic storm of activity, anxiety and busyness. This is not restricted to commercial markets, news and social media. The storm blows within the Church: obsession with activism, exponential numerical growth and ambition are symptoms of this. Radcliffe suggests that sleep is a 'time of the Spirit' and that just as the parable reminds the farmer that in spite of all his work and worry the seed sprouts and grows while he sleeps, so 'in the Church we need to do a bit more sleeping, trusting in the Lord of the harvest'.

The freneticism of a sleep-deprived society sees those sleeping, watching and praying in the midst of a busy world as either grossly irresponsible or missing out on a fast-moving world. To an outside observer, those inside the Church are dozing off. This is not just about prayer, but it is an ecclesiological issue too: the Church might be viewed as dozing off and burying her head so as not to confront the storm. The concept of *theosomnia*, in which people succumb to hallowed sleep and prayer, draws from the Galilee storm, and at the heart of it Jesus is fast asleep. The sleeping Christ counters freneticism.

This takes us to the ethics of sleep. The obsession with busyness is the playing of a power game, and there is a theological danger inherent in that. Pastors must be alert to the possibility that lack of sleep, projected as a reflection of busyness, can be a sign of the dangers of indispensability. Sleep can be deployed in different ways to project power – *I do not need it*, or *I can sleep as much as I like because I am powerful*. The British Prime Minister in the 1980s, Margaret Thatcher, famously existed on little sleep. She sought to give the impression that sleep was for the faint hearted; as she said in her memoirs *The Downing Street Years*, 'there is an intensity about being Prime Minister which made sleep seem a luxury. In any case I trained myself to do with about four hours a night.' It is as if she were saying 'I am so indispensable, I don't need it'.

Sleep can be used as a means of projecting power and countering the rhythms of day and night, sleeping and waking. Some of this is driven by technology which affects sleep patterns, but it also plays to a Babel-like attempt to achieve domination through ignoring those rhythms. We will now consider some of the implications of this societal situation and connect it with the theological themes of our exploration of theology and sleep.

Consequences of theosomnia

Hallowing the day

Through the *temporale*, Christian liturgy marks the rhythms and charts the patterns of the Christian liturgical year as they unfold the mysteries of the Christian faith, for example at Christmas the incarnation and Easter, the resurrection. Every so often come the interjections in the *sanctorale* of particular feasts and celebrations, which elucidate further aspects and insights of Christian living, usually through the celebration of the saints. This is a familiar concept, if not generally thought about, for many Christians. The Liturgy of the Hours intensifies that pattern into a daily focus, seeking to sanctify the moments, or Hours, of the day and night. Classically this is the monastic sevenfold pattern, that is condensed in other traditions. It is from the tradition that many Anglicans are familiar with the collect of the Book of Common Prayer at evensong that prays to 'lighten our darkness, we beseech thee, O Lord; and of thy great mercy defend us from all perils and dangers of this night...' A little less well known is the prayer from Matins which gives thanks to God, 'who hast safely brought us to the beginning of this day'. Even less well known is the prayer in *Common Worship: Daily Prayer*, inspired by Lancelot Andrewes (1555–1626), which includes these words:

> As your dawn renews the face of the earth
> bringing light and life to all creation,
> may we rejoice in this day you have made;
> as we wake refreshed from the depths of sleep,
> open our eyes to behold your presence
> and strengthen our hands to do your will,
> that the world may rejoice and give you praise.[3]

All these prayers connect with a theosomniac reading of the way in which going to sleep, being asleep and waking are marked and hallowed. It is my primary contention that a theological consideration of sleep should reignite the practices of prayer before bed and on waking, whether that is informally or through reengaging with the traditional practices of the Church.

Stay awake!

The second contention is that through a theological reengagement with parables that deploy sleep as a key image there can be a more expansive understanding and application of those parables. The parables, which are more often than not pointing to life in, and anticipation of, the Kingdom of God, interrogate the way in which we live now. The conclusion so often enjoins the hearer to 'stay awake', to 'be awake', which invites the hearer to consider whether or not they are indeed awake to, and to what they might be asleep. It also connects us with the experience of the disciples in Gethsemane who were taken over by sleep at a critical juncture. The example of the wise bridesmaids (Matthew 25) leads us to consider how we sleep in a state of readiness and alert to the possibilities of the waking life. It is what Benedict articulates in his *Rule*, which as we have seen directs monks to sleep fully clothed so that they are ready to wake and to go to prayer.

---

3   *Common Worship: Daily Prayer*, p.110.

Pastoral care

Pastoral care is a key element of the Church's ministry. It is first and foremost directed to the lost, the weak and the vulnerable. As far as sleep is concerned, more and more people in a modern 24/7 society are becoming exposed to sleep patterns that are not good for their wellbeing, both mental and physical. My third contention is that a good theology of sleep commends care of the whole person, body, mind and spirit, and eschews a body–soul dualism because it is the whole person who sleeps. This has practical implications.

The workplace

Commending and modelling a good relationship between work and sleep is something the Church can offer, but it is something that Church meetings and activities going on late into evening do not always encourage. This demands that the Church honours the rhythms which flow from a doctrine of creation, and that are reflected in the *temporale* and the Liturgy of the Hours. For Christians the Sabbath requirements have been reworked through the New Testament such that they are made for the person, not the person for them (cf. Mark 2.27). This means that rest, which includes sleep, is a virtuous act deriving from God's purpose in creation.

Sleep is not sloth. Good sleep benefits work life and is not an intrusion into productivity, but if anything benefits it. The Church would do well to have in mind the text 'it is in vain that you rise up early and go late to rest, eating the bread of anxious toil' (Psalm 127.2). A theosomniac Church resists the societal impulse never to rest, always to be active, because as the psalm verse continues, 'for he gives sleep to his beloved'.

Relationships

Many pastors observe at different stages of life the pressures that poor sleep can bring to the way in which people relate to one another. This is an area where good theosomniac teaching can make a difference. Whilst parents of young children are almost certainly not going to be able to sleep the consolidated sleep patterns they were used to before having children, they might still be encouraged to reflect on how they relate to their offspring when their sleep is broken. Offering comfort to a child who has suffered a night terror reflects the watchfulness of God. The act of tucking a child into bed and assuring them of safety speaks of God's protection over the vulnerable. Praying with and for the sleeping child becomes an act of vigil and watchfulness. The same could be applied to the care of the elderly too. And this is at the cost of the one who gives that care, but that is something that the watchful pastor, parent or child will do.

Commending sleep for adolescents and young adults is also profoundly important. Whilst sleep patterns will not be those of their parents, poor sleep hygiene engendered by unhealthy relationships with alcohol, drugs or mobile devices is of developmental and social concern. Tiredness not only reduces academic performance and work productivity, but it can also impair relationships and diminish understanding. This is a challenge for parent and teenager alike, and is something that Church youth workers would do well to focus on in their work.

Grief and care of the bereaved

The Church has many points of contact with the bereaved. For them sleep is very often elusive or problematic. Grief can breed restlessness from an acute sense of loss and impulse to search for the beloved. We can see this in the grieving Mary Magdalene whose behaviour is suggestive of insomnia brought on by grief as she comes to the tomb of Jesus early in the morning. Homiletics sees this searching as evocative of the lover in the Song of Songs seeking out the beloved: the insomnia of grief is the insomnia of love.

Sleep can also serve to intensify the loss that has been experienced. In her book *The Empty Bed*, Susan Wallbank writes about the death of a partner or spouse and bereavement and the loss of love. 'Sleeping with' a spouse is not simply euphemistic. No longer sleeping with a partner, as in being in the same bed, is a particularly acute expression of bereavement. She describes how the bed, focuses loss of sexual contact but also the intimacy of some of the pre-sleep practices that might have been shared. Those practices of cuddling up or a kiss goodnight that would have presaged sleep cannot now happen and so sleep is disrupted. The place of intimacy – but also rest, refreshment and sleep – becomes a place where the elusiveness of sleep is magnified. Wallbank describes the overwhelming nature of the size of a double bed when no longer occupied by two people and strategies to overcome that sense: 'Much of the work of speculation and confrontation, of deep thought and painful feelings, of hopes and fears, of dreams and despair, takes places in the quiet night hours as we lie alone in our unshared bed.' Yearning for sleep mirrors the yearning for the person who has died.

The time of sleep highlights loneliness in a way that is not quite the same during the waking hours of the day. Wallbank comments that 'we are most open to thoughts and feelings in the quietness of the night... All of the defences that help us through the day, slip from us at night.' Indeed in grief at all stages, dreams or nightmares can disturb sleep. It is no surprise that the sheer physicality of grief affects sleep, which is itself a physical act. The pastor is well advised to enquire after the quality or existence of the bereaved person's sleep as an indicator of their wellbeing: absence of sleep leads to deep tiredness and indicates profound loneliness. The pastor is also mindful that the decisions that need to be made after a bereavement are significant ones and should only be made when the grief is less acute and sleep is less disrupted.

Mental health and wellbeing

Sleep and mental health have a complex relationship, and mental health has not been well understood by society or the Church arguably throughout human history. There is a pressing imperative for pastors to become more adept at understanding mental health, and in the context of this book in its relationship with sleep. That is not to say that the connections have not been made before in the Christian tradition. Andrew Solomon, writing from personal experience on depression in particular and mental health in general, calls his book *The Noonday Demon*. That title is a quote from the Vulgate translation of one of the psalms of Compline, Psalm 91:

> You will not fear the terror of the night,
> Not the arrow that flies by day,
> Nor the pestilence that stalks in the darkness
> Nor the demon that lays waste at noonday.

Solomon recognises the connection between day and night, and sleep and insomnia, made in those verses. Older traditions of interpretation, amongst them Cassian, connected the 'noonday demon' to melancholia. Melancholia is exposed by the brightest part of the day, rather than relying on the cover of night. Melancholia may be what we now know as depression.

Frank Lake describes the Gordian knot of conflicting pressures of sleep and depression and the difficulties of finding ways to address it. Lake clinically connects insomnia to the 'relaxation of super-ego activity'. As Lake and other writers know, alcohol anaesthetises some of the anxiety and pressure of the waking day, but adversely affects the sleep it seeks to induce. Job's experience articulates this:

> Amid thoughts from visions of the night,
> When deep sleep falls on mortals,
> Dread came upon me, and trembling,
> Which made my bones shake...
> Between morning and evening they are destroyed;
> They perish forever without any regarding it. (Job 4.13, 14, 20)

In Lake's words, falling asleep is reminiscent of 'the surrender of one's own introspective awareness of self-hood as well as of other people'. That is why it is so reassuring to have another person present, a light on or a reminder of the love of God when falling asleep. Sleep heightens the fear of annihilation. Andrew Solomon recalls valuing 'my parents' good night kisses, and I used to sleep with my head on a tissue that would catch them if they fell off my face'. Solomon's description of sleep medication suggests fleeting respite and not a real addressing of the issues of his poor mental health and its relationship to sleep.

The relationship between sleep and mental health is an intricate one and not clear cut. Justice cannot be done to it here. However, Andrew Solomon makes points that are pertinent to sleep and pastoral care. For example, both oversleep and lack of sleep are features of depression. This is not equivocation on his part, but illustrative that 'sleep hygiene' is compromised in depression. It raises the question as to whether or not poor sleep can lead to depression, or if depression leads to poor sleep. The answer is complex and unresolved, and different types of depression have different sleep patterns. Not all poor sleep implies depression or mental health problems. As Solomon notes, everyone can wake up with an ominous sense of dread, and that this 'fearful despairing state...may be the closest that healthy people come to the experience of depression'. This is the spectrum of 'grey states between full-blown depression and a "mild ache"', of which changes in sleep patterns are a factor. Medication distorts sleep, either to induce it or prevent it.

This has real pastoral implications for Christian pastors, parents and friends. Solomon details the hormonal, chemical and neurotransmitter factors that affect sleep and some of the ways that it can be addressed but also asks acute questions of society: could society-wide depression be related to the decreased amounts of sleep, historically speaking, that people now have? This is reflected in the concerns already raised about sleep patterns in the young relating to technology and social media as well as those working long or anti-social hours, such as shift-working. Little is really known about depression, and similarly what sleep is for, and perhaps even less about the interconnection of the two. Nonetheless, pastoral care demands that attention is given to both.

This takes us back to Jonah: his sleep is not atypical of someone with depression or panic attack, such is the compromised and conflicted state of his life. Jonah slept through a storm, with a sleep (Andrew Solomon records having slept for 50 hours at a time whilst on medication). James Alison's interpretation of Jonah's sleep further connects it to depression. He sees Jonah's shame as causing turbulence – literally and figuratively – something Jonah had not acknowledged, 'and so can't act out of the calm of one who is loved'. Furthermore, Alison suggests that on waking from his sleep Jonah is 'wakened only at one level of his being'. Into this complex relationship of sleep, mental health and pastoral care, pastors can offer to the troubled the calm of knowing that that person is loved and to seek to awaken them at more than one level of who they are, to understand the depth and dimensions of their lives so as not to be defined by poor mental health and, like Lazarus awakened from the tomb, be unbound to life in its abundance.

Speaking of death

As we saw in Chapter 3, Christian language around death and sleep has very porous boundaries. This can be confusing. We saw instances – the Raising of Lazarus and Jairus' daughter – where sleep referred to death and a 'death' was exposed as sleep. We also saw the apostle Paul's use of 'sleep' to refer to death as benign and deprived of its sting. The danger of this language is that removed from its theological context such language quickly slips away from metaphor and back to euphemism. In theosomniac terms, the way in which we speak of death and sleep has to be handled carefully; to detach the two takes each out of its Christian theological framework. When the two are detached, the chronic affliction of humanity, fear of mortality, is thrown into sharp relief. My fourth contention is that theology needs to recover this language and re-appropriate it in a way that speaks as a contemporary apologetic for a Christian understanding of death.

On being mortal and denying death

Atul Gawande has written and spoken on dying and death and the care, or lack of, which surrounds it.[4] Gawande's argument, simply put, is that death in particular, and life in general, has become over-medicalised because modern western society cannot face mortality in a positive way. The earlier work of Elisabeth Kübler-Ross is well known in seminaries.[5] Her description of stages of grief is an invaluable tool in understanding the journey of grief and different features of it and stands the test of time. Equally significant is her conviction, like Gawande's, that facing death with all its anxieties, fears and hopes is not something to be shied away from. It is this pastoral concern to enable good and healthy conversation around death that makes her work so powerful.

Kübler-Ross addresses some of the language and actions that surround death which detract from that ability to face the awful finality of death. She gives as examples the application of makeup of a dead body or the removal of the body from the home to be dealt with remotely at a funeral parlour. These are practices that deflect the reality of death without diminishing the fear of it. This is corrosive because it means what is faced is not really death. At the heart of what Gawande and Kübler-Ross are saying, in different ways, is that it is healthy for mortality to be faced honestly (and that this is good for those who will grieve).

---

4   Gawande, A. (2014) *Being Mortal: Illness, Medicine, and What Matters in the End.* London: Profile Books.

5   Kübler-Ross, E. (1970) *On Death and Dying.* London: Tavistock.

One of the ways in which death is masked, she suggests, is in the way it has been associated with sleep. She recalls an incident from her childhood in Switzerland in the 1930s of a farmer who had been injured in an accident. The farmer wanted to die at home, and no one thought to deny him that. He died in his bed, his place of sleep, surrounded by his family, having been visited by neighbours in the village. Kübler-Ross's point is that 'in that country today there is still no make-believe slumber room, no embalming, no false make up to pretend sleep'. The fact that children were still about, engaged in conversation and seeing the body of the deceased, 'gives them the feeling that they are not alone in grief and offers them the comfort of shared responsibility and shared mourning'. This contrasts with a society where death is regarded as a taboo or, as Gawande argues, seen as a failure, and that death is 'too much' for children, and adults except the close family, who have to bear the death alone. It is in the context of the problems of grief deferred that Kübler-Ross argues that excuses for a death are both misleading and damaging, for example 'Mother has gone on a long trip', or 'God loves little boys so much that he took Johnny to heaven'. Predating Gawande, but on the same trajectory, she notes that the greater the contemporary scientific advance, the more death is feared and denied. Euphemisms and making 'the dead look as if they were asleep' all adds to this.

The difficulties of the language of sleep and death are sharply articulated by Tessa Wilkinson. She urges extreme caution about what is said to children, especially when a sibling has died:

> For example, to say: 'he has fallen asleep' or 'God wanted him more than we did' or, even more equivocally, 'he's gone on a long holiday', may lead to problems and traumas in the future. Saying 'He has fallen asleep' may lead to a fear of going to sleep from which there is no waking up.[6]

That, and Kübler-Ross's point about making the dead look asleep, would seem to suggest that 'sleep' is a wholly inappropriate image to use when referring to death. Wilkinson adds, however, that 'whatever expression is used or whatever explanation is given, it should be one

---

6   Wilkinson, T. (1991) *The Death of a Child: A Book for Families*. London: Julia MacRae Books.

which parents afterwards feel able to support or develop, because it is rooted in their beliefs or their understanding of death'. This is perhaps the point: a casual use by Christians of the language of sleep and death detached from a Pauline understanding of 1 Corinthians 15 (which is not helped by the bowdlerising tendencies of the NRSV as seen in Chapter 3) reintroduces a euphemism that seeks to diminish the fear of mortality but only succeeds in making it more acute.

Rest in peace

The use of the term 'rest in peace' is an example of Christian language mutating in the wider, and less theologically educated, environment. The prayer of the Requiem Mass, *requiescat in pace*, has become the acronym 'RIP'. This is well suited to social media for its brevity, but with little understanding of what rest is being asked for and what the nature of that peace is. In 2017 the Protestant Orange Order in Northern Ireland issued a warning to its members to stop using 'RIP' on messages of condolence because of its Catholic associations with prayer for the dead. In that sense they were historically correct if ecumenically archaic. It raises the question of how we speak of and pray for the dead and what we think we are doing.

Of course, Lazarus was not left to rest in peace in the tomb, but was summoned out and was unbound. The account of Lazarus intersects the reality of death and mortality with sleep and grief. So what of all that? Andrew Lincoln captures the significance of this scene: 'talk of Lazarus's death as sleeping suggests not only the reversibility of that death but also that the believing dead, whom Lazarus represents, will be awakened by Jesus to life at the final resurrection'. This is the radical origin of sleep/death theological language: Jesus has power over life and death. As Marianne Meye Thompson notes, '[Jesus] knows that Lazarus is only sleeping and that the whole incident is an occasion for the manifestation of God's glory.'

Therefore, as *theosomniacs*, we should insistently articulate that the Christian language of sleep and death is not the denial of mortality but rather the embracing of it in the 'sure and certain hope of the resurrection to eternal life', as the Funeral Service puts it. This is to root it in the Christian hope of 'the life of the world to come' (Nicene Creed).

The sleeping place

Throughout this book I have sought to show Christian theology expressed not only in writing but in prayer, hymnody and practice. In some ways the account of the practices has been word based, for example looking at the texts of prayers and hymns, albeit, and this is the point, that the prayers and hymns are prayed at intentional times associated with sleeping and waking. One very obvious embodied practice is that of burial and rites around death.

Radcliffe illustrates the early Christian connection of life, sleeping and death reflected in the practices around early Christian burial. This is no denial of mortality brought on through the language of sleep. Christian burial moved the dead from being buried beyond the limits of Rome, first in the catacombs and then by the fifth-century graveyards within the city. This was an expression of solidarity in death within the communion of saints and that the body was hallowed and not polluting, contrary to earlier Roman notions of burial. Radcliffe sees this move as a 'slow-motion fulfilment of Matthew's account of the consequence of Christ's resurrection' (Matthew 27.52–53), in which we read of tombs being opened in the aftermath of the death of Jesus, 'and many bodies of the saints who had fallen asleep…raised'. He goes on to note that, 'by the Middle Ages, virtually every Church was surrounded by the dead. They were not buried in a *necropolis*, literally a "city of the dead", but a *cemetery*, which means a place to sleep, a dormitory, awaiting the Kingdom.'

This is how and why the Church of England and the Roman Catholic Church use a prayer in common at funerals of 'Entrusting and Commending' that says: '*N* has fallen asleep in the peace of Christ…' In prayers for funerals the following texts appear: 'For those who have fallen asleep in the hope of rising again, that they may see God face to face'; and, drawing on Matthew 27, 'Judge of the living and the dead, at your voice the tombs will open and all the just who sleep in your peace will rise and sing the glory of God.'

This is hope and confidence in the face of mortality and a robust conviction that the death is no more.

'I commune with my heart in the night'

'I sleep, yet my heart wakes'

This book has been predicated on the assumption that, up until this point, there has been no systematic theology of sleep articulated. I have endeavoured to begin that task. No doubt others will add to it. My final contention is that sleep naturally locates itself within pastoral and mystical theology. I have argued that there is an operating theology of sleep in devotional material and hymnody, and so I will close with excerpts of notes that I made after staying at a convent on retreat, during which I rose in the night, at 2.30 a.m., to watch and pray. These notes were written the following day and bring together many of the themes of this book.

Something I have found to be a source of great comfort to those who cannot sleep is for them to know that they are being prayed for. As I wrote in my journal during that retreat:

> Yet so many [other people] are awake too: all those suffering from the distress of war, the displaced; those in perils; travellers. Such a comprehensive list made me more aware, as I prayed, of the diversity of life and human society and its needs. Waking in the night opens up new vistas of prayer. Is it always sleep we need, or is it prayer? My inconvenience, albeit intentional, of waking is nothing compared to those at a death bed; identifying a dead body at the morgue; sitting on their bed contemplating not God, but contemplating the ending of their life. I prayed for the sleeping, working, those lying awake, and those tempted to sin: drug dealing, burgling, deceiving, 'sleeping' with someone in their bed by lust or force. I had the joy of praying for those being born, for new mothers and midwives.

This expresses the solidarity of prayer with all who go to that familiar yet deeply strange place, the place we call sleep.

And so I wrote:

> The alarm went off. I woke. I felt refreshingly alert. I had gone to sleep early, straight after compline, having already prepared the place where I would pray. It was at a *prie dieu* in the other room. There was a crucifix, an icon and a candle. I had set out a prayer stool with the order of service and an intercessions list.

I made my way from my bedroom to where I would pray, in the small amount of light that seeped through from the bedside lamp. It was not pitch black, but dark enough that when I struck the match to light the candle the flash of light flared and momentarily lit up the room. *Lighten our darkness we beseech thee, O Lord.* Breaking sleep broke the darkness with the created, and inadequate, light of the candle. The uncreated light of Christ shines in the darkness.

I was intensely aware of my body, which had switched from the depths of sleep into a quite different mode. I felt almost more prepared than normal. The posture helped, i.e. the prayer stool, and I had made a point of wearing a cross around my neck. *Take up your cross daily and follow me...*

The 'tea-light' candle needed lifting up like a lantern. So I lifted it up on a saucer. The candle did not light the whole room. It cast an inconvenient shadow and had to be in exactly the right position to illuminate the order of service. The candle placed by the icon on the top of the *prie dieu* was insufficient for reading the order of service. Indeed, as soon as I got to elements I knew by heart I put the candle down: *Your word is a lantern to my feet and a light upon my path* (Psalm 119.105).

Whilst I was aware of my body, the impact of the words was considerable. Phrases referring to light, darkness, sleep, night etc. were predictably, perhaps, ringing with connections, but also familiar texts in a new setting, context, were very powerful. The Trisagion [holy God, holy and strong, holy and immortal] made the very floor tremble, and was deeply stirring to my body that was moving from deep sleep. This bodily awareness made *St Patrick's Breastplate* touch me in a new way. It moved from head to heart: *Christ be with me* (in the darkness), *Christ within me...Christ beside me* (as I pray with you 'beside' me in my bed)...*Christ in quiet, Christ in danger* (whose danger? Mine or his? He is with me in danger, but I was with him in the darkness of the night in which he was betrayed. But I had been a sleeping disciple prior to waking. I was too weak, too late to bed with me in his danger, like Peter I trailed in late).

On rising from sleep, we fall down before you. That was exactly it! As was *You have roused me, Lord, from my bed and sleep...* I had been roused from my bed… In the darkness the light, poor as it was, felt more searching than I have known before: *You have searched me out and known me, You know my sitting down and rising* (Psalm 139.1). In the darkness you see me more clearly, if that is possible, or, at least, I see more clearly that you are with me. This is my meditation in the watches of the night.

I read Psalm 3, the psalm of someone waking in adversity. As I was waking up I wondered what a waking/sleeping 24/7 world would make of what I was doing, *how many there are who say, 'There is no help for you in your God'* (Psalm 3.2). Stephen Hawking had said on the television the previous day that belief in the afterlife was a 'fairy story for people afraid of the dark'.[7] He combined two strands of Psalm 3, ridicule and the night.

I lie down and sleep and rise again, because the Lord sustains me (Psalm 3.5). Yes, that night I lay down, I rose up again with the benefit of the iPhone alarm. But, waking, deliberately, in the night raised bigger questions than in the morning. After all, in the morning I can rejoice in the gift of the new day and get on with it. At night I am going to lie back down on my bed and seek sleep. Where had I been when I was asleep, unconscious, and 'dead to the world'? I was not there. I was not waking to breathe, pump blood, digest, perspire etc. but I was doing it. Where was I? What *is* it, then, that sustains me? …*the Lord sustains me*…waking and sleeping. Just as the seed grows whilst the farmer worries, sleeps and rises, so I continue to live and change.

If sleep anticipates death at all then I face it confident that in the life of the world to come *the Lord sustains me*. Since, as Paul says, *nothing, not even death, can separate us from the love of God* (Romans 8.38, 39).

The psalm also led me into the Paschal Mystery of the Exodus. *Rise up, O Lord; set me free, O my God* (Psalm 3.7). The plea that the Lord will be awake to my cry and, by the Holy Spirit, free me into all the truth. How the Spirit does that exceeds the expectation of

---

7   'Dara O Briain meets Stephen Hawking', 12 June 2015. http://www.bbc.co.uk/programmes/p02tjndb, accessed 15 June 2015.

the psalmist. Yes, regrettably, enemies are struck, drowned, no less, in the Red Sea. The people moved and escaped by night, led by the pillar of fire. My Night Prayer was a pale shadow of the vigils of Maundy Thursday and the Triduum but centred on God, and so I knew afresh, in the night, *deliverance belongs to the Lord*, I could claim *his blessing* (Psalm 3.8)…

A special prayer to me concluded the intercession: 'Keep watch, dear Lord…and give your angels charge over those who sleep…' And then mindful of God's great mercy, the Kyries. The final collect took me back to the eternal beginning, *Let there be light*. I had lit my candle some ten minutes before, but by rising in the dead of night had felt the pulse of another rhythm throbbing in the world. This was the rhythm of day and night, morning and evening, inaugurated by the Creator, Logos and Spirit, which brooded over the waters in the beginning and whispered, *Let there be light. And there was light* (Genesis 1.3).

In that light I returned to bed. Hold thou thy cross before my closing eyes. I sleep, but my heart wakes.

BIBLIOGRAPHY

1995 Catechism of the Catholic Church (Pocket Edition). London and Rome: Geoffrey Chapman – Libereria Editrice Vaticana.

Abraham, W.J. (2015) 'Foreword.' In J.R. Farris and C. Taliaferro (eds) *The Ashgate Research Companion to Theological Anthropology*. Farnham: Ashgate.

Adams, N. (2007) 'Pelagianism: Can People be Saved by Their Own Efforts?' In B. Quash and M. Ward (eds). *Heresies and How to Avoid Them: Why it Matters What Christians Believe*. London: SPCK.

Archbishops' Council, The (2000) *Common Worship Services and Prayers for the Church of England*. London: Church House Publishing.

Archbishops' Council, The (2007) *Common Worship: Daily Prayer*. London: Church House Publishing.

Archbishops' Council, The (2007) *Common Worship: Ordination Services Study Edition*. London: Church House Publishing.

Archbishops' Council, The (2007) *Common Worship: Pastoral Services*. London: Church House Publishing.

Archbishops' Council, The (2007) *Common Worship: Times and Seasons*. London: Church House Publishing.

Alison, J. (1997) *Living in the End Times: The Last Things Re-Imagined*. London: SPCK.

Alison, J. (2001) *Faith Beyond Resentment: Fragments Catholic and Gay*. London: Darton, Longman and Todd.

Alison, J. (2010) *Broken Hearts and New Creations: Intimations of a Great Reversal*. London: Darton, Longman and Todd.

Ancoli-Israel, S. (2003) 'Sleep disorders in the Bible.' *Jewish Bible Quarterly 31*, 3. Accessed 31 May 2014 at http://jbq.jewishbible.org/assets/Uploads/313/313_Sleepfil.pdf

Anderson, A.A. (1972) *The Book of Psalms: Volume 2*. Grand Rapids, MI: Eerdmans.

Anderson, R.S. (1986) *Theology, Death and Dying*. Oxford: Basil Blackwell.

Bachelard, G. (1958, 1969) *The Poetics of Space*, trans. M. Jolas. Boston, MA: Beacon Press.

Baillie, J. (1961) *Christian Devotion: Addresses by John Baillie*. London: Oxford University Press.

Balthasar, H.U. von (1968) *Man in History: A Theological Study*. London: Sheed and Ward.

Barrett, C.K. (1971) *The First Epistle to the Corinthians*. London: A & C Black.

Barth, K. (1933) *The Epistle to the Romans*, trans. E.C. Hoskyns. Oxford: Oxford University Press.

Barth, K. (1960, 2004) *Church Dogmatics. Volume III.2: The Doctrine of Creation*. London: Continuum.

Bernard of Clairvaux, St (1951) *On the Song of Songs* (*Sermones in Cantica Canticorum*). Translated and edited by A Religious of CSMV. London: Mowbray.

Best, E. (1986, revised edition) *The First and Second Epistles to the Thessalonians*. London: A & C Black.

Bishops' Conference of England and Wales (1991) *Order of Christian Funerals*. London: Geoffrey Chapman.

Blackwell, B.C. and Miller, K.A. (2015) 'Theosis and Theological Anthropology.' In F.R. Farris and C. Taliaferro (eds) *The Ashgate Research Companion to Theological Anthropology*. Farnham: Ashgate.

Body and Society (2008) Special Issue on Sleeping Bodies. *Body and Society 14*, 4.

Bonhoeffer, D. (1954) *Life Together*, trans. J.W. Doberstein. London: SCM Press.

Brown, D. (2007) *God and Grace of Body: Sacrament in Ordinary*. Oxford: Oxford University Press.

Brown, R.E. (1970) *The Gospel according to John XII–XXI*. New York: Doubleday.

Brown, R.E. (1996) *The Gospel according to John I–XII*. New York: Doubleday.

Brown, W.S. and Strawn, B.D. (2012) *The Physical Nature of Christian Life: Neuroscience, Psychology and the Church*. Cambridge: Cambridge University Press.

Browne, T. (1963) *Religio Medici*, ed. J. Winney. Cambridge: Cambridge University Press.

Burridge, R. (1998) *John*. Abingdon: Bible Reading Fellowship.

Cary, P. (2008) *Jonah*. London: SCM Press.

Caussade, J-P. (1933) *Self-Abandonment to Divine Providence*, ed. P.H. Rannieère, trans. A. Thorold. London: Burns, Oates and Washbourne.

Chadwick, H. (trans.) (1991) *Saint Augustine: Confessions*. Oxford: Oxford University Press.

Chesterton, G.K. (2003) *Father Brown: Selected Stories*. London: Collector's Library.

Coakley, S. (2002) *Powers and Submissions: Spirituality, Philosophy and Gender*. Oxford: Blackwell.

Coakley, S. (2013) *God, Sexuality, and the Self: An Essay 'On the Trinity'*. Cambridge: Cambridge University Press.

Coe, J. (1997) *House of Sleep*. London: Penguin.

Cortez, M. (2015) 'The Madness in Our Method: Christology as the Necessary Starting Point for Theological Anthropology.' In J.R. Farris and C. Taliaferro (eds) *The Ashgate Research Companion to Theological Anthropology*. Farnham: Ashgate.

Cottrell, S. (2012) *Christ in the Wilderness: Reflections on the Paintings by Stanley Spencer*. London: SPCK.

Crary, J. (2013) *24/7: Late Capitalism and the Ends of Sleep*. London: Verso.

Crisp, O. (2015) 'A Christological Model of the *Imago Dei*.' In J.R. Farris and C. Taliaferro (eds) *The Ashgate Research Companion to Theological Anthropology*. Farnham: Ashgate.

Cyril of Jerusalem, *Catechetical Lectures XIV*, 17.

Davis, S.T. (2015) 'Redemption, the Resurrected Body, and Human Nature.' In J.R. Farris and C. Taliaferro (eds) *The Ashgate Research Companion to Theological Anthropology*. Farnham: Ashgate.

Davison, A. (2013) *The Love of Wisdom: An Introduction to Philosophy for Theologians*. London: SCM Press.

Dement, W.C. (1972) *Some Must Watch While Some Must Sleep*. San Francisco: W.H. Freeman.

De Waal, E. (1995) *A Life Giving Way: A Commentary on the Rule of St Benedict*. London: Mowbray.

Doja, A. (2014) 'Socializing enchantment: a socio-anthropological approach to infant-directed singing, music education and cultural socialization.' *International Review of the Aesthetics and Sociology of Music 45*, 1, 115–147.

Drury, J. (2013) *Music at Midnight: The Life and Poetry of George Herbert.* London: Penguin Books.

Edgar, T.R. (1979) 'The meaning of "sleep" in 1 Thessalonians 5.10.' *Journal of the Evangelical Theological Society 22,* 4, 345–349.

Ekirch, A.R. (2005) *At Day's Close: A History of Nighttime.* London: Weidenfeld and Nicolson.

Elias, N. (1939, 1978) *The Civilising Process. Volume One: The History of Manners.* Oxford: Blackwell.

Farmer, D.H. (1965/1983) *The Age of Bede.* London: Penguin.

Foster, R. (1989) *Celebration of Discipline: The Path to Spiritual Growth.* London: Hodder and Stoughton.

Foucault, M. (1977) *Discipline and Punish: The Birth of the Prison.* London: Tavistock.

Fox, D. (2013) 'The Secret Life of the Brain.' In J. Webb (ed.) *Nothing: From Absolute Zero to Cosmic Oblivion – Amazing Insight into Nothingness.* London: Profile Books.

Gawande, A. (2014) *Being Mortal: Illness, Medicine, and What Matters in the End.* London: Profile Books.

Gebara, I. and Bingemer, M. (1989) *Mary, Mother of God, Mother of the Poor,* trans. P. Berryman. Maryknoll NY: Orbis Books.

Geddes, L. (2013) 'Banishing Consciousness.' In J. Webb (ed.) *Nothing: From Absolute Zero to Cosmic Oblivion – Amazing Insight into Nothingness.* London: Profile Books.

Green, J.B. (2008) *Body, Soul and Human Life: The Nature of Humanity in the Bible.* Grand Rapids, MI: Baker Academic.

Green, J.B. (ed.) (2004) *What About the Soul? Neuroscience and Christian Anthropology.* Nashville: Abingdon Press.

Green, J.B. (2015) 'Why the *Imago Dei* Should Not Be Identified with the Soul.' In J.R. Farris and C. Taliaferro (eds) *The Ashgate Research Companion to Theological Anthropology.* Farnham: Ashgate.

Guite, M. (2016) 'The Pains of Sleep: Coleridge on Prayer.' Accessed 26 February 2016. https://malcolmguite.wordpress.com/2016/02/26/the-pains-of-sleep-coleridge-on-prayer

Gutenson, C.E. (2004) 'Time, Eternity and Personal Identity: The Implications of Trinitarian Theology.' In J.B. Green (ed.) *What About the Soul? Neuroscience and Christian Anthropology.* Nashville: Abingdon Press.

Hardy, A. (1979) *The Spiritual Nature of Man: A Study of Contemporary Religious Experience.* Oxford: Oxford University Press.

Harrison, V. (2010) *God's Many Splendored Image: Theological Anthropology for Christian Formation.* Grand Rapids, MI: Baker Academic.

Hauerwas, S. (2006) *Matthew.* London: SCM Press.

Herbert, G. (1995) *The Complete English Works,* ed. A. Pasternak Slater. London: David Campbell Publishers.

Hertzberg, H.W. (1964) *I & II Samuel: A Commentary.* London: SCM Press.

Hippolytus of Rome, 'The Refutation of All Heresies', Book 10, Chapter 29. Accessed 26 June 2015 at http://www.documentacatholicaomnia.eu/03d/0180-0254,_Hippolytus_Romanus,_The_Refutation_Of_All_Heresies_[Schaff],_EN.pdf

Hobson, J.A. (2002) *Dreaming: A Very Short Introduction.* Oxford: Oxford University Press.

Horne, J. (1988) *Why We Sleep: The Functions of Sleep in Humans and Other Mammals.* Oxford: Oxford University Press.

Hughes, G.W. (1985) *God of Surprises.* London: Darton, Longman and Todd.

Irenaeus of Lyon, 'Demonstration of Apostolic Preaching.' Accessed 29 June 2015 at http://www.ccel.org/ccel/irenaeus/demonstr.preaching_the_demonstration_of_the_apostolic_preaching.html.

Irvine, C. (2013) *The Cross and Creation in Christian Liturgy and Art*. London: SPCK Alcuin.

Israel, M. (1990) *Night Thoughts*. London: SPCK.

Ivens, M. (1998) *Understanding the Spiritual Exercises*. Leominster: Gracewing.

Jacobs, S. (2012) 'Ambivalent Attitudes Towards Sleep in World Religions.' In A. Green and A. Westcombe (eds) *Sleep: Multi-Professional Perspectives*. London: Jessica Kingsley Publishers.

Jeeves, M. (2004) 'Mind Reading and Soul Searching in the Twenty-first Century.' In J. Green (ed.) *What About the Soul? Neuroscience and Christian Anthropology*. Nashville: Abingdon Press.

Jeeves, M. (2005) 'Neuroscience, evolutionary psychology, and the image of God.' *Perspectives on Science and Christian Faith 57*.

Jeffrey, D.L. (2012) *Luke*. Grand Rapids, MI: Brazos.

Jenson, R.W. (2009) *Ezekiel*. London: SCM Press.

Jerome, *In Ionam Prophetam*. Accessed 15 February 2014 at http://www.johnsanidopoulos.com/2009/09/prophet-jonah-in-writings-of-church.html

Johnson, L.T. (1992) *The Acts of the Apostles*. Collegeville, MI: The Liturgical Press.

Jones, D.G. (2004) 'A Neurobiological Portrait of the Human Person: Finding a Context for Approaching the Brain.' In J. Green (ed.). *What About the Soul? Neuroscience and Christian Anthropology*. Nashville: Abingdon Press.

Jowett, N. (2013) 'A theology of slumber.' *Church Times*, 14 February 2013. Accessed 5 August 2015 at http://www.churchtimes.co.uk/articles/2014/14-february/comment/opinion/a-theology-of-slumber

Kingsmill, E. (2014) 'The Hart and the Gazelle.' In *Fairacres Chronicle 47*, 2.28–37.

Kirk, K.E. (1931) *The Vision of God: The Christian Doctrine of the Summum Bonum*. Cambridge: James Clark.

Kübler-Ross, E. (1970) *On Death and Dying*. London: Tavistock.

Lake, F. (1966) *Clinical Theology: A Theological and Psychiatric Basis to Clinical Pastoral Care*. London: Darton, Longman and Todd.

Leder, D. (1990) *The Absent Body*. Chicago: University of Chicago Press.

Lee, N. (2008) 'Awake, asleep, adult, child: an a-humanist account of persons.' *Body and Society 14*, 4, 57–76.

Levi, P. (1984) *The Penguin Book of English Christian Verse*. London: Penguin.

Lincoln, A.T. (2008) 'The Lazarus Story: A Literary Perspective.' In R. Bauckham and C. Mosser. (eds) *The Gospel of John and Christian Theology*. Grand Rapids, MI: Eerdmans.

Linn, D., Fabricant Linn, S. and Linn, M. (1995) *Sleeping with Bread: Holding What Gives You Life*. Mahwah, NJ: Paulist Press.

Lipton, D. (2009) *Revisions of the Night: Politics and Promises in the Patriarchal Dreams of Genesis*. London: Continuum.

Lisieux, Thérèse of (1988) *Critical Edition of the Complete Works of St Thérèse of Lisieux: General Correspondence, Volume 2, 1890–1897* (trans). Clarke, J. Washington DC: ICS Publications.

Lisieux, Thérèse of (1996) *Story of a Soul: The Autobiography of Thérèse of Lisieux*, trans. J. Clarke. Washington DC: ICS Publications.

Lockley, S.W. and Foster, R.G. (2012) *Sleep: A Very Short Introduction*. Oxford: Oxford University Press.

Luibhied, C. (trans.) (1985) *John Cassian: Conferences*. Mahwah, NJ: Paulist Press.

Luibhied, C. and Russell, N. (trans.) (1982) *John Climacus: The Ladder of Divine Ascent*. London: SPCK Publishing.

McAlpine, T.H. (1987) *Sleep, Human and Divine, in the Old Testament*. Sheffield: JSOT Press.

McGilchrist, I. (2010) *The Master and His Emissary: The Divided Brain and the Making of the Western World*. New Haven and London: Yale University Press.

McGinn, B. (1994) *The Growth of Mysticism: From Gregory the Great to the Twelfth Century*. London: SCM Press.

Maitland, S. (2008) *A Book of Silence: A Journey in Search of the Pleasures and Powers of Silence*. London: Granta.

Maquet, P., Smith, C. and Stickgold, R. (2003) *Sleep and Brain Plasticity*. Oxford: Oxford University Press.

Martin, J. (2012) *The Jesuit Guide to (Almost) Everything: A Spirituality for Real Life*. New York: HarperCollins.

Melbin, M. (1978) 'Night as frontier.' *American Sociological Review* 43, 1, 3–22.

Melville, H. (1992) *Moby-Dick; or, The Whale*. London: Penguin Books.

Merleau-Ponty, M. (1992) *Phenomenology of Perception*. London: Routledge.

Merton, T. (1963) *New Seeds of Contemplation*. New York: New Directions.

Metzger, B.M., Denton, R.C. and Harrelson, W. (1991) *The Making of the New Revised Standard Version of the Bible*. Grand Rapids, MI: Eerdmans.

Moltmann, J. (1996) *The Coming of God: Christian Eschatology*. London: SCM Press.

Moltmann, J. (1998) *Is There Life After Death?* Milwaukee, WI: Marquette University Press.

Morgan Wortham, S. (2013) *The Poetics of Sleep: From Aristotle to Nancy*. London: Bloomsbury.

Moritz, J.M. (2015) 'Evolutionary Biology and Theological Anthropology. In J.R. Farris and C. Taliaferro (eds) *The Ashgate Research Companion to Theological Anthropology*. Farnham: Ashgate.

Murray, P. (2002) *A Journey with Jonah: The Spirituality of Bewilderment*. Dublin: The Columba Press.

Naipaul, V.S. (1990) *India: A Million Mutinies Now*. London: William Heinemann.

Nancy, J-L. (2009) *The Fall of Sleep*, trans. C. Mandell. New York: Fordham University Press.

Nicholl, M. (1950) *The New Man: An Interpretation of Some Parables and Miracles of Christ*. London: Penguin.

Northcott, M.S. (2004) 'Being Silent: Time in the Spirit.' In S. Hauerwas and S. Wells, (eds) *The Blackwell Companion to Christian Ethics*. Oxford: Blackwell.

Nyssa, Gregory of, *On the Making of Man*, Limovia.net

Pelikan, J. (2006) *Acts*. London: SCM Press.

Peterson, C. and Seligman, M.E.P. (eds) (2004) *Character Strengths and Virtues: A Handbook and Classification*. Oxford: Oxford University Press.

Prestidge, W. (2010) *Life, Death and Destiny*. Warren Prestidge (eBook).

Quash, B. (2012) *Abiding*. London: Bloomsbury Publishing.

Radcliffe, T. (2012) *Taking the Plunge: Living Baptism and Confirmation*. London: Bloomsbury.

Rahner, K. (1967) *Theological Investigations (III): Theology of the Spiritual Life*, (trans.) K-H. and B. Kruger. London: Darton, Longman and Todd.

Rahner, K. (2010) *A Theology of Everyday Life*, ed. S.A. Kidder. Maryknoll, NY: Orbis.

Ramsey, M. (1949) *The Glory of God and the Transfiguration of Christ*. London: Libra.

Ratzinger, J. (1988) *Eschatology: Death and Eternal Life*. Washington DC: Catholic University of America Press.

Rilke, R.M. (2013) *Prayers of a Young Poet*, trans. by M. Burrows. Brewster, MA: Paraclete Press.

Ross, M. (2014) *Silence: A User's Guide*. London: Darton, Longman and Todd.

Rowell, G., Stevenson, K. and Williams, R. (2001) *Love's Redeeming Work: The Anglican Quest for Holiness*. Oxford: Oxford University Press.

Sanders, F. (2002) The Daily Scriptorium Blog 'The Theology of Sleep.' Accessed on 29 June 2015 at http://scriptoriumdaily.com/the-theology-of-sleep

Scott, D. (2001) *Sacred Tongues: The Golden Age of Spiritual Writing*. London: SPCK.

Slade, H. (1977) *Contemplative Intimacy*. London: Darton, Longman and Todd.

Smith, J.K.A. (2013) *Imagining the Kingdom: How Worship Works*. Grand Rapids, MI: Baker Academic.

Solomon, A. (2014) *The Noonday Demon: An Anatomy of Depression*. London: Vintage.

Stackhouse, I. (2008) *The Day is Yours: Slow Spirituality in a Fast-Moving World*. Milton Keynes: Paternoster.

Steindl-Rast, D. and Lebell, S. (1998, 2002) *Music of Silence: A Sacred Journey Through the Hours of the Day*. Berkeley, CA: Ulysses Press.

Steiner, G. (1996) *No Passion Spent: Essays 1978–1996*. London: Faber and Faber.

Summers, S. (1998) 'Out of my Mind for God': a social-scientific approach to Pauline pneumatology'. *Journal of Pentecostal Theology 13*, 77–106.

Taylor-Johnson, F. 'Sleep: 2002.' Accessed on 24 June 2015 at http://samtaylorjohnson.com/photography/art/sleep-2002

Thiselton, A.C. (2000) *The First Epistle to the Corinthians*. Grand Rapids, MI: Eerdmans.

Thiselton, A.C. (2012) *The Last Things: A New Approach*. London: SPCK.

Thompson, M.M. (2008) 'The Raising of Lazarus in John 11.' In R. Bauckham and C. Mosser (eds) *The Gospel of John and Christian Theology*. Grand Rapids, MI: Eerdmans.

Trehub, S.E. and Trainor, L. (1999) 'Singing to Infants: Lullabies and Play Songs.' In C. Rovee-Collier and L.P. Lipsitt *Advances in Infancy Research 12*, 43–69.

Twain, M. (2009) *Diaries of Adam and Eve*. London: Oneworld Classics.

Verney, S. (1985) *Water into Wine: An Introduction to John's Gospel*. London: Darton, Longman and Todd.

Visala, A. (2015) 'Theological Anthropology and the Cognitive Sciences.' In J.R. Farris and C. Taliaferro (eds) *The Ashgate Research Companion to Theological Anthropology*. Farnham: Ashgate.

Vogüe, A. de (1977, 1983) *The Rule of St Benedict: A Doctrinal and Spiritual Commentary*, ed. J.B. Hasbrouck. Kalamazoo, MI: Cistercian Publications.

Wallbank, S. (1992, 2005) *The Empty Bed: Bereavement and the Loss of Love*. London: Darton, Longman and Todd.

Ward, G. (2014) *Unbelievable: Why We Believe and Why We Don't*. London: I.B. Tauris.

Ward, H. (1989) *The Gift of Self*. London: Darton, Longman and Todd.

Ware, K. (2000) *The Inner Kingdom*. New York: St Vladimir's Seminary Press.

Ware, K. (2002) '"The Earthly Heaven" – The Mother of God in the Teaching of St John of Damascus.' In W. McLoughlin and J. Pinnock (eds) *Mary for Earth and Heaven: Essays on Mary and Ecumenism*. Leominster: Gracewing.

Warren, J. (2007) *Head Trip: A Fantastic Romp Through 24 Hours in the Life of Your Brain*. Oxford: Oneworld.

Wells, S. (2004) *Improvisation: The Drama of Christian Ethics*. London: SPCK.

Wilkinson, T. (1991) *The Death of a Child: A Book for Families*. London: Julia MacRae Books.

Williams, R. (2000) *On Christian Theology*. Oxford: Blackwell.

Williams, R. (2002) *Ponder These Things: Praying with Icons of the Virgin*: Norwich: Canterbury Press.

Williams, R. (2004) 'The Christian Priest Today': lecture on the occasion of the 150th anniversary of Ripon College, Cuddesdon. Accessed 24 June 2013 at http://rowanwilliams.archbishopofcanterbury.org/articles.php/2097

Williams, R. (2014) *The Edge of Words: God and the Habits of Language*. London: Bloomsbury.

Williams, S.J. (2005) *Sleep and Society: Sociological Ventures into the (Un)known*. Abingdon: Routledge.

Williams, S.J. (2011) *The Politics of Sleep: Governing (Un)consciousness in the Late Modern Age*. Basingstoke: Palgrave Macmillan.

Williams, S.J. and Crossley, N. (2008) 'Introduction: sleeping bodies.' *Body and Society* *14*, 4, 1–13.

Wright, N.T. (2003) *The Resurrection of the Son of God*. London: SPCK.

Wright, T. (2002) *Matthew for Everyone: Part 2, Chapters 16–28*. London: SPCK.

Ziesler, J. (1989) *Paul's Letter to the Romans*. London: SCM Press.

SUBJECT INDEX

AUTHOR INDEX

The Revd Canon Dr Andrew Bishop is a Residentiary Canon of Guildford Cathedral and Anglican and Coordinating Chaplain to the University of Surrey, Guildford, UK. Ordained in the Church of England in 1996, Andrew has also served as a parish priest in Central London and Basingstoke. Following an Masters in Pastoral Theology at Heythrop College, London, he was awarded a Doctorate in Theology and Ministry by King's College, London in 2012. His doctoral thesis formed the basis of his book *Eucharist Shaping and Herbert's* Liturgy and Society: *Church, Mission and Personhood* (2016). Andrew's interest in sleep research began at the University of Surrey in 2013 since when he has engaged in inter-disciplinary work as well as writing articles, leading retreats, quiet days and conferences on the subject of sleep and theology.